White Britain and Black Ireland

The Influence of Stereotypes on Colonial Policy

A Publication of the
Institute for the
Study of Human Issues

ISHI is a nonprofit research organization that promotes work in the behavioral, natural and social sciences and in the humanities. It was founded in the belief that scholars can best pursue their research when freed from the constraints of traditional academic structures.

Since ISHI is committed to the unrestricted dissemination of knowledge, its policy is to make public the results of all its members' investigations. It refuses to engage in classified research, or in any research whose results cannot be publicly circulated. In addition, ISHI has developed a publishing program, of which this book is a part, to make available significant works of scholarship.

RICHARD NED LEBOW

White Britain
and
Black Ireland

The Influence of Stereotypes
on Colonial Policy

A Publication of the
Institute for the Study of Human Issues
Philadelphia

Set in ComCom Baskerville type and printed in the
United States of America by the Haddon Craftsmen

Designed by Joseph Lebow

Library of Congress Cataloging in Publication Data:

Lebow, Richard Ned.
    White Britain and Black Ireland.

    Bibliography: p.
    Includes index.
    1. Irish question. I. Title.
DA950.2.L4   941.5081   75-41333
ISBN 0-915980-01-0

For information, write:

Director of Publications
ISHI
3401 Science Center
Philadelphia, Pennsylvania 19104

To W. A. M.

Contents

Introduction

The phenomenon of colonialism has been investigated carefully in the decades following the Second World War. Most studies have approached it as a key stage in the development of non-Western areas. Scholars have asked: What can we learn about newly independent countries by studying the impact of colonialism upon them? Recent research on Asian and African states has analyzed their new elites in terms of the educational and economic innovations of the Western powers; the prevalent ideology and goals have been considered as a response to colonial rule and the political forms as creations of the struggle for independence. The colonial experience is envisaged as the crucible in which the new societies were molded. However, if colonialism has been decisive for the maturation of a new East, its failure and collapse have been equally instrumental in the growth of a new West. Yet scholars have generally neglected to ask: What can we learn about Europe by studying colonialism from the European perspective?

This has not always been the case. An earlier generation of scholars, alive to the possibilities offered by such study, sought a clearer understanding of their own society by investigating European colonial expansion. Hobson and Lenin ventured to lay bare the structure of European capitalism by examining the financial relationships between the metropolitan powers and their colonies. Joseph Schumpeter sought to illuminate the impact of social classes on European politics by means of a sociological analysis of imperial ambitions. William

Langer undertook a historical investigation of the diplomacy of imperialism with the hope of providing insights into the nature of European political rivalries. These pioneering studies and the later scholarship generated by them have unquestionably added a new dimension to our understanding of nineteenth-century Europe.[1]

While these studies of colonialism differ greatly in method and conclusion, all attempt to analyze the roots of colonial expansion. When this research was first undertaken colonialism appeared to be approaching its zenith. The last decades of the nineteenth century witnessed the extension of European power to all corners of the world. Predicated upon a dynamism and a degree of military, economic and administrative superiority never before achieved by one culture over another, the new systems of colonial empire appeared to most contemporary observers to be a novel but lasting feature of the international system. Even the Marxists, who predicted the collapse of colonial empire, assumed that a progressive but nevertheless paternalistic form of leadership would continue to be exercised over colonial peoples until they reached a higher stage of development. Accordingly, scholars desired to understand what appeared to be one of the most significant developments of recent times.

Today the era of colonial empire is over and with it the age of European ascendancy. Most colonies have become independent and assert their equality before their former masters. From the vantage point of the late twentieth century we cannot help but have an altered perspective on colonial empire. The most important feature of colonialism in light of contemporary political realities is no longer its origin and development but rather its failure and decline. Such a change in perspective dictates a corresponding shift in scholarly focus. The investigation of the underlying reasons for the collapse of colonial empire should prove as fruitful to our understanding of Europe as the analysis of empire's origins did to a former generation of scholars. It is to this aspect of the colonial period that this study is directed. It will analyze British perceptions of the Irish during the first half of the nineteenth century. By doing so the author hopes to illuminate the causes for Britain's failure in Ireland. In the last chapter an attempt will be made to relate the lessons of Ireland to other countries and other colonial relationships.

Note

1. V. I. Lenin, *Imperialism: The Highest Stage of Capitalism* (New York, 1939); John A. Hobson, *Imperialism: A Study* (Ann Arbor, 1965); Joseph Schumpeter, *Imperialism and Social Classes*, trans. Heinz Norden (New York, 1951); William Langer, *The Diplomacy of Imperialism* (New York, 1935).

CHAPTER 1

The Irish
Political Background

> *If there are strong tendencies toward eventual failure
> inherent in all autonomous organizations, and
> particularly governments—as many pessimistic theories
> of politics allege—then such difficulties can perhaps be
> traced to their propensity to prefer self-referrent
> symbols to new information from the outside world.*
>
> KARL DEUTSCH

The Act of Union of 1800 marked a significant change in British policy toward Ireland. Henceforth Britain's goal with respect to Ireland became integration. Partisans on both sides of the Irish Sea hoped that the amalgamation of the two countries would be the prelude to a new era of Anglo-Irish relations characterized by reconciliation and cooperation. The structure of the Union encouraged such optimism. The eight articles which embodied the political, commercial and religious basis of the Union were not intrinsically unfair to Ireland. Assuming that they would be administered in a spirit of justice, one had reason to suspect that the Union, like the Anglo-

Scottish Union a century before, would prove beneficial to both countries.

The most important provisions of the act were the first four articles, which established the political basis of the Union. Ireland was to be united with Great Britain in one kingdom, to be known as the United Kingdom of Great Britain and Ireland. The Irish parliament in Dublin was to be disbanded but in its place Ireland was to receive representation in the British parliament: thirty-two seats in the House of Lords and one hundred seats in the House of Commons, almost one-fifth of the whole.

The remaining articles enumerated the religious and economic settlement. The Church of England was to be united with the Church of Ireland and the maintenance of the united church was deemed to be "an essential and fundamental part of the Union." Irish subjects were accorded the same freedom of trade and commerce exercised by citizens of Great Britain. Free trade was established between the two countries with the important qualification that duties were to be maintained for twenty years on certain categories of manufactured goods. Finally, the act provided for independent financial systems for the two countries. Each was to have its own exchequer and national debt and to contribute to the general expenses of the kingdom in the proportion of two parts for Ireland and fifteen parts for Great Britain. This proportion was to be reconsidered after twenty years and thereafter could be altered by act of Parliament.

The great inequality that remained between the two countries and threatened to make a sham of the Union was represented by the existing British legislation barring Catholics from holding most political offices, including membership in either house of Parliament. While the franchise in Ireland was comparatively liberal—more liberal than in Britain—continued exclusion of Catholics from office threatened to make the Union nothing more than a settlement between Great Britain and the Protestant minority which for centuries had held all the reins of political authority in Ireland. However,

Castlereagh, an architect of the Union, promised to correct this injustice as a quid pro quo for Irish approval of the Union. By 1840 most Catholic Irishmen were thoroughly disillusioned with the Union and denounced it as a repetition of the old pattern of exploitation and indifference, albeit under a new guise. "Emancipation"—the granting of political rights to Catholics—although promised by Pitt and Castlereagh, was not awarded until 1829 and even then was robbed of much of its significance by the simultaneous disenfranchisement of the forty-shilling freeholders, the very voters upon whom Catholic politicians would rely for support. The obstinacy and bigotry that marked the fight against emancipation was equally evident in the British response to other Irish problems. The Union was consistently administered in a manner designed to secure British advantage at Irish expense.

By far the greatest contradiction between the promise held out by the Union and its actual results lay in the economic sphere. Ireland was exploited as a market for British goods and as a source of cheap labor and capital to help finance British industrial growth. The commercial clauses of the Act of Union, in theory designed to provide an impetus for Irish economic development, in practice enabled British manufacturers to hamper Irish industry and trade. After 1815 British manufacturers, responding to a depression at home, dumped their surplus goods on the Irish market, now no longer protected by tariffs. Most Irish industries, smaller in scale than their British counterparts, did not have the economic resilience to survive such competition. The cumulative effect of these actions, unchecked by any legislation protecting Irish interests, so depressed the economic condition of the country that numerous contemporary observers were forced to conclude that the Irish people were the most impoverished in all of Europe. This increasing pauperization of Ireland was all the more dramatic when contrasted with earlier British assurances that the Union would promote Irish prosperity.

The general British failure to respond to Irish needs provoked a growing political reaction against the Union. This reaction was characterized by two distinct approaches to achieving justice for Ireland. The first, that of the Loyal National Repeal Association and its predecessor, the Catholic Association, was reformist in nature and predicated upon the belief that the Irish could secure redress of their grievances by parliamentary means. In the pre-famine years of the early 1840s the Repeal Association, an alliance of Catholic intellectuals with the Catholic urban middle class and the more prosperous peasantry, was in the forefront of the Irish agitation. Repealers demanded far-reaching legislative reforms and, failing that, repeal of the Act of Union and the re-establishment of an Irish parliament in Dublin.

The guiding spirit behind the agitation was Daniel O'Connell, known as the "Liberator" to the masses of Ireland. A lawyer from County Kerry, O'Connell was both a liberal and a Catholic, an unusual combination for his time. He was active in a variety of radical causes and won national prominence for his speeches in favor of parliamentary reform and repeal of the Corn Laws. O'Connell's liberalism was probably responsible for his optimistic assessment of the possibility for Anglo-Irish reconciliation, for along with other Victorian liberals he perceived the ultimate triumph of democratic principles to be almost inevitable. He was convinced that as such principles became ascendant the contradiction between them and British policy toward Ireland would force the government to bring its policy into tune with the spirit of the age. However, the steadily deteriorating condition of Ireland demanded more immediate action and O'Connell hoped to hasten the slow pace of reform by employing a judicious combination of moral appeal and political pressure.

With this end in mind O'Connell and his supporters organized the Repeal Association to provide Irish reformers with an effective political base. By 1843 the Repeal Association had become the preeminent political force in Ireland. Repealers had enrolled over two million members, had created their own press and had established reading rooms in the countryside where illiterate peasants were taught to read and were given

"RINT" *v.* POTATOES.—THE IRISH JEREMY DIDDLER.

O'Connell is demanding of the woman with hungry children: "You haven't got such a thing as Twelve-pence about you?—A Farthing a week—a Penny a month—a Shilling a year?" To support the movement O'Connell collected "Repeal rent" of a penny a month from peasants as well as larger contributions from more affluent Catholics. For this imaginative fund-raising the cartoon compares him to Jeremy Diddler, a swindler in an early nineteenth-century farce. From *Punch* (1845).

a political education. The association held numerous political rallies, known as "monster meetings," where well-known Repealers lashed out at British injustices and sought to demonstrate the extent of their popular support to legislators in London. Within Parliament the two dozen Repeal representatives, claiming to speak in the name of the masses of Ireland, proposed a series of legislative reforms and appealed to the British people and government to alleviate the inequalities that prevailed in Ireland. Hopeful that reform could be achieved within the existing political framework or by repeal of the Union, Repealers were careful to shun violence and keep their agitation within what they considered to be proper constitutional bounds.

The second element of the political agitation, represented by the Young Ireland movement, was characterized by a more pessimistic view of Anglo-Irish reconciliation. Centered around the *Nation,* a radical Dublin newspaper, the movement attracted young Protestant and Catholic intellectuals schooled in the politics of Repeal but disillusioned by the association's apparent failure to secure significant reform for Ireland. The two movements were separated by profound differences of ideology and style. O'Connell was a reformer in the tradition of Curran and Grattan; he aspired to restore the traditional rights of Ireland which he believed had systematically been encroached upon by the British Crown and Parliament. Young Irelanders rejected the validity of this approach. They subscribed to an organic view of the Irish nation; they saw the country as a being with its own individuality, whose rights could be neither alienated nor compromised. Taking their cue from similar movements on the Continent, these romantic nationalists stressed the uniqueness of Ireland and emphasized its history, language and culture. They traced their political lineage through earlier Irish rebels, most notably the United Irishmen of 1798. While O'Connell believed that Ireland's future was closely tied to Britain's, Young Irelanders were convinced that independence was the only proper solution to the "Irish question."

In the years between 1800 and 1916 the Union's potential for success depended upon Britain's ability to respond effectively to the demands of the Irish moderates, so as to win the support of the emerging Catholic middle class. The failure of successive governments to do this undermined the appeal of the constitutional moderates, such as the Repeal Association and later the Irish Parliamentary Party, and made the nationalist solution of independence advocated by Young Ireland attractive to growing numbers of Irishmen. Gradually the balance of power in Ireland was reversed, as the revolutionary nationalists gained support at the expense of the nonviolent parliamentarians. Young Ireland, though crushed in the abortive revolution of 1848, was the progenitor of the Fenians, the terrorists of the sixties who, in turn, paved the way for Sinn Fein, the Easter Rebellion and ultimately civil war and independence.

With the benefit of historical hindsight it is easy to trace the shift of Irish support from constitutional agitation to revolutionary action and correspondingly difficult to understand why the British leadership was unable or unwilling to initiate the reforms that would have placated the moderates, outflanked the revolutionary nationalists and created a secure basis of support for the Union. With the exception of some prominent intellectuals and a small number of politicians, the most notable of whom was Gladstone, the British political elite refused to endorse willingly any concessions to Irish demands. Rather, reforms like Catholic emancipation were granted only when they were perceived as necessary to forestall revolution. At the same time British leaders were unwilling to espouse the truly draconian measures required to prevent a counterelite from preparing for revolution in Ireland. Such a policy, which neither won Irish support nor effectively suppressed Irish dissidence, was doomed to failure.

Why did successive British governments pursue such a counterproductive policy toward Ireland? Why was the government unable or unwilling to respond effectively to the demands of either the Irish Catholic middle class or the peasantry? It is doubtless true that certain powerful interests profited from the maintenance of the status quo in Ireland. Nevertheless, these interests, the big Protestant landowners, the established church and some manufacturers, might not have been able to dictate Irish policy if sufficient numbers of Englishmen had become aroused over the injustice of it. The public failed to develop empathy for the plight of the Irish people—even when faced with appeals for support and exposed to information detailing the Irish condition. Why was this so?

CHAPTER 2

The Theory
of Prejudice

> *How can an elite of usurpers . . . establish their
> privileges? By one means only: debasing the colonized
> to exalt themselves, denying the title of humanity to
> the natives, and defining them as simply absences of
> qualities—animals, not humans. This does not prove
> hard to do, for the system deprives them of everything.*
>
> JEAN PAUL SARTRE

The contemporary literature on prejudice is rooted in Freud's
classical explanation of this phenomenon as an expression of
repressed libidinal impulses.[1] Psychologists following Freud
have sought to establish links between prejudice and feelings
of frustration, guilt and fear. One common hypothesis, the
theory of direct projection, asserts that ethnic hostility is a
projection of unacceptable inner strivings onto a minority
group. By projecting such impulses (for instance, sexual
desire, greed, indolence) onto other persons and "punishing"
them for these supposed attributes, a person may alleviate

13

his own anxieties.[2] This formulation may be expressed as follows:

Repression
Guilt (Anxiety)
Projection
Expressions of Hostility
Release

While psychologists have focused on the individual personality, sociologists and historians have applied Freudian theory to classes and groups. They have noted, for example, a high association between expressions of prejudice and socioeconomic change. Expressions of prejudice, measured by any index, are more pronounced in periods of economic distress and are most apparent among groups or classes who perceive their status to be threatened by change. The anxiety generated by change may find release in expressions of hostility against out-groups whether or not these groups in fact constitute a threat.[3]

According to this view ethnic and so-called racial prejudice, while by no means a solely modern phenomenon, has been especially pronounced during the nineteenth and twentieth centuries because of the rapid social and economic transformation of the Western world and the insecurities this change has generated. The ebb and flow of anti-Semitism in central Europe and anti-Black prejudice in the United States can be cited as examples. In both cases the prejudice appeared to be more pronounced among those classes most adversely affected by the modernization process. Expressions of prejudice were also most apparent during times of economic distress.[4]

Recently L. P. Curtis, Jr., has employed this formulation to explain racist attitudes toward the Irish in Victorian Britain.[5] Curtis draws a parallel between the apparent upsurge of racism in Britain and the growth of anti-Semitism on the Continent. In both cases he suggests that the minority in question provided a scapegoat for classes whose values and position were most severely threatened by modernization.

Upon close examination the Curtis argument is found wanting in several ways. While it is likely that industrialization aggravated anti-Irish prejudice among certain classes, such prejudice was by no means limited to those classes whose position was most threatened by either the ongoing transformation of Britain or competition with cheap Irish labor. Rather, anti-Irish sentiment was widespread among almost all segments of the British population. More important, widespread and virulent expressions of anti-Irish prejudice predate the industrial revolution. They had been part of the British scene for centuries.[6] The only novelty in Victorian times was the fact that the prejudice was increasingly articulated in the terminology of racial differentiation. Racist expressions were merely the age-old anti-Irish prejudice couched in the jargon of the day. In this author's opinion the Victorian attitude was in no way qualitatively distinct from the derision and fear of the Irish which preceded it. Indeed, an argument can be made that anti-Irish sentiment in Britain actually declined in the second half of the nineteenth century. The scholar must therefore look for an alternate explanation for the origin of British prejudice toward the Irish.

Moral Codes and Rationalizations

All societies develop moral codes to regulate the social behavior of their members. These codes are justified in the name of some supernatural being or in reference to a set of sacrosanct principles. The members of any society are more or less imperfectly socialized into accepting the validity of its ethical imperatives and into conforming to its corresponding behavioral norms. To the extent that the code becomes internalized by a person it becomes difficult for him to violate it without suffering guilt or anxiety. If he becomes very conscious of the disparity between his behavior and the internalized moral code the anxiety can reach an intolerable level. In such cases psychologists argue that the anxiety must be reduced if the person is to function effectively.[7]

There can be little doubt that the treatment of the native populations of European colonies flagrantly violated the behavioral norms of the metropolitan societies. This can be seen by examining the structure of colonial relationships. Many students of colonialism have defined the colonial situation in reference to two conditions which, they believe, differentiate it from other political relationships. They are: (1) the loss of autonomy on the part of the indigenous inhabitants of the colony and (2) the exploitation of the colony in the interests of the metropolitan power. A colonial situation develops when a political system achieves domination over another society by reason of its military, economic and administrative superiority and uses that power to exploit the wealth, human resources and geographical position of the colony. Political power is usually exercised by a minority of settlers, soldiers and administrators who represent the colonizing country and are placed as trustees over the fate and fortunes of the inhabitants. Their function is to maintain the presence of the colonial nation while pursuing policies designed to increase the power and wealth of that society.[8]

Historically, the indigenous inhabitants of colonies have been treated as superfluous beings impeding the designs of the colonizer or as additional "capital" to be exploited along with the other resources of the territory. The British colonization of North America is an example of the first type of behavior. The settlers desired to clear the land and farm the soil but often found the native inhabitants a barrier to this enterprise. As the colonists relentlessly expanded the area of settlement, they repeatedly pushed the Indians further into the hinterlands of the continent. Eventually most Indians were destroyed by European diseases or exterminated by the settlers.

The Spanish *padrones* in the New World pursued the other policy. They valued the Indians for the useful labor they could be made to perform. Over time, the native people were transformed into serfs and their tribal organization was destroyed. In either case, solicitude for the existence and well-being of the native inhabitants was usually demonstrated only insofar as it furthered the attainment of the colonizer's goals.

The relationship between the colonizer and the colonized was therefore fundamentally antagonistic, by reason of the superfluous or subservient role to which most of the colonial population was relegated. To the extent that the native population began to demand political rights and opportunities for economic and social mobility, conflict was bound to arise. The demands were usually unacceptable to the colonizer because they threatened to disrupt the basic political and economic structure of the colony. The military might then become not only the means through which conquest was achieved but also the means through which opposition was suppressed and rule maintained.

If, in fact, the colonizer's policies flagrantly violated the behavioral norms of the metropolitan society, we ought to be able to discern some pattern of behavior that helped to reduce the tension that arose by virtue of this contradiction. This supposition finds some support in the ideological justifications of empire advanced by the colonial powers. The justifications can be interpreted in terms of the various types of rationalizations that individuals find effective in harmonizing the contradiction between belief and behavior.

One such rationalization attempts to justify the discrepant behavior by the end it produces. We may call this the "white lie" syndrome. Lying is generally considered to be reprehensible. If, however, the lie is told for some altruistic motive, such as saving a friend from unnecessary embarrassment, it can be legitimated by emphasizing the commendable end it is meant to achieve.[9]

This type of rationalization was endemic to colonial situations. Supporters of empire have been loath to admit that some form of exploitation was the goal of colonial expansion. While not denying the advantages that accrued to them from the colonies, they sought to justify empire in terms of some higher good that would result from it. By reason of this noble end policies that might otherwise have been reprehensible became permissible.

The Spanish colonial empire is a case in point. It would be difficult to find a colonial situation in which the lust and greed of the colonizers were given freer rein or one in which greater atrocities were perpetrated against the native population. There can be no doubt that the dream of quick material profit motivated the conquistadors to carry the power of Spain to the New World. However, conquistador and king alike proclaimed the goal of empire to be the conversion of the heathen Indians to Christianity.

The moral veneer thus imparted to the Spanish empire was certainly politically efficacious in that it enabled Spain, and later Portugal, to marshal the support of the papacy behind their colonial ambitions. It also served to assuage the guilt generated by the cruel manner in which the Indians were treated. There is evidence to suggest that many Spaniards—King Ferdinand among them—were able to condone this treatment only because of the higher good which they honestly believed would result from the enterprise.[10] They envisaged the conversion of the Indians to be such a splendid and noble achievement that it more than compensated for the slaughter, rapine and oppression that accompanied it.

The idea of the "white man's burden," advanced to justify European colonial expansion in the nineteenth century, was another manifestation of this rationalization. The changed emphasis merely reflected the secularization of Europe that had occurred during the centuries spanning the two great epochs of European expansion. Now the higher good promoted by colonialism consisted of the diffusion of the benefits of Western civilization among non-European peoples. The violent subjugation of foreign territories and the authoritarian regimentation of their inhabitants were justified in terms of this noble end. The colonizer's harsh measures were defended as being in the best interests of the natives themselves.

Once again the rationalization was politically efficacious

in that it provided a defense against those critics who were agitated by the manner in which the native inhabitants were being treated. It also reduced the anxiety that developed from the contradiction between the values of the metropolitan society and the more inhumane aspects of colonial rule.[11]

Another rationalization commonly employed to harmonize the contradiction between values and behavior is the redefinition of the behavior as a special case in which the moral code is inapplicable. The people toward whom reprehensible actions are directed are differentiated by criteria that place them outside the realm in which the moral code is thought to apply. For example, the stereotypical European merchant would not cheat his regular customers but overcharges foreign tourists. Since the tourists are foreign they are beyond the pale of his moral code. Perhaps he sees them as so wealthy that they can afford to overpay. In any case some rationalization is employed to differentiate them from the merchant's compatriots.

The differentiation process can operate in colonial situations. It most frequently involves some attempt to "dehumanize" the indigenous population of the colony. If the population can thus be differentiated from oneself, it is not difficult to argue that a code of behavior unacceptable among one's peers can be applied without qualms to the natives. The most obvious example of this rationalization is once again found in the Spanish colonial empire.

Throughout the sixteenth century a great debate was waged in Spain over the question of whether the Indians were human beings. A majority of the conquistadors and plantation owners argued that, while the Indians resembled humans in form, they were really animals. It followed from this premise that there was nothing wrong in treating them like beasts of burden—a fair description of their status in the colonies.

The opponents of this view, who were mostly members of the clergy, were shocked by the treatment of the Indians and fought to protect them against the worst abuses. They argued that Indians possessed souls and were therefore human; if they did not have souls how could Spain embark upon a mission to

Christianize them? This proved to be a telling argument and resulted in a papal bull affirming the human status of the Indians.

A similar debate took place among the British settlers in North America. From the earliest days of settlement colonists were divided in their attitude toward the Indians. Many colonists and, later, frontiersmen declared the Indians to be inhuman savages. When considered as mere animals they could be treated like other pests that interfered with human enterprise; they could be deprived of their land and even their existence without much remorse.

The later stereotyped images of African and Asian peoples were yet another example of this rationalization. By the nineteenth century it was no longer possible to describe these peoples as nonhuman. Instead, metropolitan societies resorted to the next best alternative. Supporters of colonialism characterized colonial subjects as backward children, thus differentiating them from Europeans. With this supposed difference they justified the divergence of the moral, legal and political codes that were applied to colonizer and colonized.[12]

Stereotypes and Cognitive Dissonance

Both the differentiation process and the rationalization of the civilizing mission ultimately rested upon a stereotype of the native that stressed his childlike state and his possession of traits usually attributed to children. It is not inconceivable that over time such an image could come to dominate perception and provide the framework by which information about the indigenous inhabitants of the colony was organized and given meaning. Several nineteenth-century observers, commenting on the apparent inability of the British people and government to admit the justice of the Irish demands, thought that such a process had indeed occurred.[13] John Stuart Mill ventured to suggest that a closed image of Ireland clouded the minds of even well-meaning individuals and was largely responsible for the peculiar blindness that Englishmen seemed to have with respect to that country.[14] To what extent was his charge justified?

The idea of a closed image, or stereotype, is a curiously elusive concept that has found a variety of interesting and often contradictory meanings among social scientists. The term "stereotype" was first employed in a psychological context by Walter Lippmann in 1922. He defined it as a form of perception that "imposes a certain character on the data of our senses before the data reach intelligence," thus implying the operation of some refractive medium through which information must pass before it takes on meaning.[15] Later researchers have interpreted this idea of a perceptive screen in two different ways. One group of social psychologists has employed it in a purely cognitive way; they stress the human need to simplify and categorize data received from the senses in order to derive a meaningful picture of reality. For them, all our images are stereotyped because they are never an accurate description of reality; rather, they are abstract representations that emphasize what appear to us to be the salient characteristics of the environment.[16]

The second general application of the concept of the stercotype has been motivational. Social scientists employing the concept in this manner have analyzed the psychoeconomic function of images which persist in light of contradictory data. They suggest that such stereotypes permit the release of tension that threatens to tear the personality structure asunder. The release is often achieved through verbal or physical aggression against groups that can be differentiated on an ethnic, national, religious or racial basis.[17] In summing up the results of research on prejudice, Howard Ehrlich writes:

> To the social psychologist, stereotypes, as the language of prejudice, are thought to provide a vocabulary of motives both for individuals and the concerted action of prejudiced persons. They signal the socially approved and accessible targets for the

release of hostility and aggression, and they provide the rationalizations for prejudiced attitudes and discriminatory behavior.[18]

Stereotypes therefore function as a special language in the discourse of prejudiced persons, a language that reinforces the beliefs of its adherents and furnishes the basis for the development and maintenance of solidarity among the prejudiced.

If stereotypes can facilitate the expression of hostility and aggression, they may also function as a kind of perceptual blinder, protecting the personality from information likely to produce internal stress. Harold Isaacs suggests that the Western stereotype of the "faceless" Chinese served such a function: it was developed by Europeans as a response to the horrible suffering they observed in China. The stereotype, which incorporated the belief that the Chinese were inured to suffering, unmindful of poverty and generally content with their lot, helped Westerners to overcome the uneasiness they felt by reason of the disparity between their affluence and Chinese poverty.[19] Stereotypes of the poor in our own country, which often explain poverty in terms of indolence or moral laxity, probably serve a similar function.

This theme is congruent with Leon Festinger's concept of cognitive dissonance. Festinger's basic contention is that "consonance" or consistency is valued over "dissonance" or inconsistency. Dissonance, he suggests, makes individuals uncomfortable and creates internal stress that they seek to reduce. For instance, confirmed cigarette smokers experience dissonance when they read reports that smoking is harmful to their health. Those smokers who are unable or unwilling to "kick" the habit but cannot escape from constant warnings about its ill-effects—now printed on every packet of cigarettes—are likely to suffer dissonance they will seek to reduce. Festinger and others have investigated the means through which the reduction can be achieved.[20]

A common means of reducing dissonance is somehow to bring the dissonant elements into harmony. The cigarette smoker, for example, can attempt to reduce dissonance by denying the validity of the information which indicates that smoking is harmful. If he can convince himself that the studies of smoking are inaccurate or based on incomplete data he can continue to enjoy tobacco without suffering from as much anxiety. It is not surprising that studies reveal that far fewer smokers than nonsmokers accept the evidence that smoking is prejudicial to good health. We can speculate that persons for whom social stereotypes serve a dissonance-reduction function are equally loath to alter their mental images. It is in this sense that the concept of the stereotype will be used in this study.

Notes

1. See Sigmund Freud, "The Neuro-Psychoses of Defense" and "Further Remarks on the Neuro-Psychoses of Defense," in *The Standard Edition of the Complete Psychological Works of Sigmund Freud* (London, 1962), Vol. III, 43–68, 159–185.

2. T. W. Adorno et al., *The Authoritarian Personality*, 2 vols. (New York, 1950); Nathan W. Ackerman and Marie Jahoda, *Anti-Semitism and Emotional Disorder: A Psychoanalytic Interpretation* (New York, 1950); and Eric Fromm, *Escape from Freedom* (New York, 1941).

3. Hannah Arendt, *The Origins of Totalitarianism* (New York, 1968); C. Vann Woodward, *The Strange Career of Jim Crow* (New York, 1955); and Gunnar Myrdal et al., *An American Dilemma: The Negro Problem and Modern Democracy* (New York, 1944).

4. Pierre Pierrard, *Juifs et catholiques français, de Drumont à Jules Isaac (1886–1945)* (Paris, 1970); Richard Levy, *Anti-Semitic Political Parties in the German Empire* (New Haven, 1969); W. F. Mandle, *Anti-Semitism and the British Union of Fascists* (London, 1968). See also the references cited in note 3.

5. L. P. Curtis, Jr., *The Anglo-Saxons and Celts: A Study of Anti-Irish Prejudice in Victorian England* (Bridgeport, Conn., 1968), and *Apes and Angels: The Irishman in Victorian Caricature* (Washington, D.C., 1971).

6. See Richard Ned Lebow, "British Historians and Irish History," *Éire-Ireland*, VIII (December 1973), 3–38.

7. Leon Festinger, *A Theory of Cognitive Dissonance* (Stanford, Calif., 1952); and Leon Festinger et al., *Conflict, Decision, and Dissonance* (Stanford, Calif., 1964).

8. See G. Balandier, "La situation coloniale: approche théorique," *Cahiers internationaux de sociologie*, XI (1961), 44–79; René Maunier, *The Sociology of the Colonies: An Introduction to the Study of a Race Contact*, trans. and ed. E. O. Lorimer (London, 1949); Octave Mannoni, *Prospero and Caliban*, trans. Pamela Powesland (New York, 1964). A striking technological disparity between the colonizer and the colonized is also implicit in most definitions of the colonial relationship.

9. For an interesting discussion of the political ramifications of such a rationalization, see Max Weber, "Politics as a Vocation," in *From Max Weber: Essays in Sociology*, trans. and ed. H. H. Gerth and C. Wright Mills (New York, 1947), 77–128.

10. Thomas F. Gosset, *Race: The History of an Idea in America* (Dallas, 1963), 12.

11. See Albert Memmi, *The Colonizer and the Colonized* (New York, 1965), 79–83.

12. William Langer, *The Diplomacy of Imperialism* (New York, 1960), Chapter III. Also see the investigation of this theme in various colonial novels: E. M. Forster, *A Passage to India* (New York, 1924); Graham Greene, *The Heart of the Matter* (London, 1948); Albert Memmi, *La statue de sel* (Paris, 1966); George Orwell, *Burmese Days* (London, 1935); Edward Douwes Dekker, *Max Havelaar, or The Coffee Sales of the Netherlands Trading Company*, trans. W. Siebenhaar (New York, 1927).

13. Daniel Dewar, *Observations on the Character, Customs, and Superstitions of the Irish . . .* (London, 1812). See also various articles in the *Nation* (Dublin) and *Westminster Review*, 1843–1845.

14. John Stuart Mill, *England and Ireland* (London, 1868).

15. Walter Lippmann, *Public Opinion*, rev. ed. (New York, 1960), 98.

16. See Rosemary Gordon, *Stereotypy of Imagery and Belief* (Cambridge, Eng., 1962) for an excellent discussion of the various meanings of stereotypes to social scientists.

17. Gordon W. Allport, *The Nature of Prejudice* (Garden City, N.Y., 1958), Parts III and IV.

18. Howard J. Ehrlich, "Stereotyping and Negro-Jewish Stereotypes," *Social Forces*, XLI, No. 2 (1962), 20.

19. Harold R. Isaacs, *Images of Asia: American Views of China and India* (New York, 1962), 99.

20. See note 7.

CHAPTER 3

The Beliefs of a Changing Britain

*The moment the very name of Ireland is mentioned,
the English seem to bid adieu to common feeling,
common prudence, and common sense.*

SYDNEY SMITH

British Values in Transition

The Anglo-Irish colonial relationship during the first half of
the nineteenth century—the fifty years following the Act of
Union—is a particularly useful case in which to search for
stereotypes and to analyze their effect on the formulation
of policy. The discrepancy between the values of British society and the means employed to preserve colonial domination
over Ireland grew steadily more apparent during that time.

Historians of Victorian Britain have pointed to the changing intellectual and moral climate as a major force in promoting the democratization of the political system.[1] This transformation of the basic value structure of British society, which
first became manifest in the years following the Napoleonic

Wars, gradually exerted its influence in the political sphere. The changing political and social concerns of the English public resulted in the waves of reform that broke over Victorian Britain.

Values clustered around the concepts of political participation, political liberty, humaneness and the ugliness of oppression motivated the social and political programs of such diverse groups as the Benthamites and the Evangelicals. As public opinion became increasingly aroused by these concepts, reformers were successful in building a consensus for legislation. General agreement as to the areas in which the liberal and humanitarian values should be applied came about very gradually; it can be argued that a full-blown legislative system was achieved only with the welfare state in the twentieth century. The first half of the nineteenth century, however, witnessed significant legislative enactments which were a harbinger of the emerging consensus.

The growing acceptance of political participation by others besides the aristocracy and squirearchy was reflected by the first Reform Act (1832), which extended the franchise and reformed the House of Commons. The goal of political liberty motivated many of the supporters of Catholic emancipation, the Jewish Disabilities Act and legislation regulating relations between church and state. The commitment to humaneness and antipathy to oppression bore fruit in prison reform, restriction of capital punishment and the reform and extension of the Poor Law. The success of the antislavery movement in the early years of the century demonstrates the strength of these attitudes all the more forcefully because the struggle to achieve antislavery legislation involved a protracted fight with important vested interests.

Political ideas at first the preserve of intellectuals gradually became accepted by the British public. As the century unfolded, the beliefs that government should be conducted in the interests of all the people, that political participation should be broad and that the state had a responsibility for the social and economic well-being of the people were becoming generally accepted dogma. Both the supporters and the opponents of specific proposals increasingly justified their positions by reference to these beliefs.

While Britain was becoming more democratic, British rule in Ireland continued to rely on force and coercion and became more *un*democratic in relation to the emerging value structure of British society. As the gulf between British principles and policy in Ireland grew wider, it also should have become more apparent to the British public, because of the incessant barrage of information and opinion concerning conditions in Ireland. Geographic proximity and a long and intimate connection between the two countries had brought about an unusually high degree of mobility of persons, ideas and information. In this sense the Anglo-Irish relationship is probably unique in the annals of colonialism.

A most significant feature of the stream of information was that a small but growing percentage of writers, analysts and politicians presented British policy in an unfavorable light. The agitation for Repeal was a case in point. Repealers attempted to confront the British people with the contradictions between their self-proclaimed goals and the actual effects of their policy.

Of overriding importance was the unusual forum presented to Ireland by the Act of Union, which awarded the country representation in both houses of Parliament as a quid pro quo for the dissolution of the Irish parliament in Dublin. After 1829 Irish Catholics, having gained the right to sit in Parliament, succeeded in capturing many of the Irish seats from the representatives of the Protestant Anglo-Irish ruling class, known as the Ascendancy. Irish politicians and their allies among the English Radicals now had an unequaled opportunity to disseminate their views throughout the kingdom. Every major newspaper and magazine carried detailed reports of parliamentary debates and proceedings, reports which at that time were the major source of political intelligence. An

Englishman reading his morning paper at breakfast was as likely as not to find before him a presentation of Irish grievances.

Therefore we have in the Anglo-Irish colonial relationship a particularly sharp disparity between values and behavior that should have been increasingly evident to the colonizers themselves. In such circumstances we should expect to find a corresponding need for rationalizations capable of reducing the dissonance created in the minds of the colonizers.

Ireland Through British Eyes

What were the images that characterized the British perception of Irishmen and Irish affairs during the first fifty years of the Union? Did they indeed reduce the dissonance that developed from the contradiction between the values of British society and that country's policy toward Ireland? Were the images stereotypes in the sense that they resisted change in light of compelling contradictory evidence? To what extent did they dominate the perception of important decision makers? Finally, what effect did such images have upon the formulation of policy?

With these questions in mind, I have explored British images of Ireland during the first half of the nineteenth century, giving special emphasis to the period between 1840 and 1846, the heyday of the agitation for repeal of the Union. The Repeal agitation is an ideal focus for the investigation because it challenged the British parliament and people to bring their policies into harmony with their professed values. Unlike a revolutionary challenge, to which the British could have responded with bayonets, the Repeal agitation stayed well within the bounds of the constitution and compelled the British to respond with words—words indicative of their view of Ireland, its inhabitants and Britain's role in that unhappy country.

To examine the British perception of Irish affairs it was important to tap a variety of sources that reflected both incoming information about Ireland and the interpretation of that information in the form of opinion about the contemporary state of affairs in Ireland. Most of these sources (for example, travel descriptions, histories, parliamentary debates) were not so numerous as to preclude a nearly complete study of the available material. For other sources (such as newspapers, journals and private papers) it was necessary to select among the available materials.[2]

The individual sources were selected in the hope that they would provide insight into the attitudes of as wide a spectrum of British society as possible, and that the resulting data could be correlated with important political, economic, religious, social and regional cleavages.* In practice it proved impossible to find sources reflecting all the diversity of British society. While those expressing elite opinion are readily available, sources expressing the attitudes of other groups on Irish affairs are not. Thus the following presentation is concerned primarily with elite opinion in both Britain and Ireland.

The opinion investigated in this study concerned the most salient aspects of the so-called Irish problem: (1) the causes of Irish poverty, (2) the nature and origin of violence in Ireland, and (3) the nature and goals of Irish political agitation (the Repeal Association). An attempt was also made to discern British images of the "national character" of the Irish people and of Britain's role in Ireland. Finally, data were collected for the period preceding 1800. The sources from which these data were drawn, primarily travel descriptions, histories and political pamphlets, were used to examine the historical continuity of British images of the Irish and of Ireland.

*The religious and geographical cleavages proved unimportant. Locale was relevant only in the sense that opinion in cities containing large numbers of Irish immigrants (for instance, London, Liverpool, Glasgow) was more anti-Irish than elsewhere.

TABLE 1   *Elements of the Study*

Sources	Histories, political pamphlets, broadsides, travel descriptions, diaries, plays and novels, newspapers, journals and magazines, parliamentary debates, parliamentary reports, official papers, private papers
Cleavages	Political faction,* economic interest, religion, class, region
Issues	General character of the Irish people, origins of Irish poverty, origin and nature of violence in Ireland, nature of political agitation (Repeal Association), Britain's role in Ireland

*During the middle years of the nineteenth century the British party system was in a state of flux. The two parties were composed of coalitions of factions, the most significant of which were the Protectionists, the Peelites, the Liberals and the Radicals.

Table 1 summarizes the sources used, the issues investigated and the cleavages with which the data were correlated. The analysis revealed three general schools of thought with respect to Irish problems. They can be characterized as follows:

1. *The Repeal Thesis.* This was the interpretation of Ireland's ills advanced by the Repeal Association and a small number of Irish Whigs. Repealers traced the ills of Ireland to the heavy yoke of British oppression. They demanded legislation to redress the worst of these grievances and, failing that, repeal of the Act of Union. Within Britain this view received qualified support from the leaders of working-class radicalism in the Midlands and from a few independent but prominent intellectuals. Since it was an extremist point of view in light of contemporary British opinion, the impact of its adherents upon the formulation of policy was insignificant.

2. *The Liberal Thesis.* The dominant model of Irish affairs, this thesis was advanced by Peelites, Liberals and many Radi-

cals and adhered to by most British newspapers and periodicals and the mass of the middle class. Spokesmen for this majority admitted that Ireland formerly had been oppressed but declared that the Union, the Irish Poor Law and other reforms had gone a long way to right the situation. Most agreed on the need for further reform but denounced repeal of the Act of Union as detrimental to both British and Irish interests. There was a striking consensus among Englishmen who adhered to this view that the major problem of Ireland was the character of its people and that prosperity and tranquility would never be achieved without a prior *moral* reformation of the native Irish.

3. *The Orange Thesis.* A minority view at the other extreme from the Repeal thesis, the Orange interpretation of Irish affairs was propagated by the Protestant Irish Ascendancy. Within Britain it received support from a vocal minority of middle-class Protestants, many of whom were especially antagonistic to Catholicism and believed the long arm of Rome to be behind the Repeal agitation. After 1830 the Orange thesis found increasing support among the partisans of what might be called the British backlash—unskilled industrial workers and agricultural laborers who felt threatened by competition from Irish immigrants, and middle-class urban Englishmen and Scots who resented the presence of large numbers of immigrant paupers in their cities. Orange spokesmen denied the existence of any real basis for Irish grievances. Instead of reform they advocated arms bills to restore "law and order" to Ireland and they called upon the government to crush the Repeal agitation. The alliance between Irish landlords and the British backlash, effective in checking reform in Ireland, threatened to break down over the question of immigration, an increasingly important issue after 1840.* Irish

---

*Before 1798 emigration from Ireland to Britain was negligible. After the Act of Union in 1800, Irish laborers, drawn largely from Leinster,

landlords fought to maintain their prerogatives with respect to the land and opposed any extension of the Poor Law; English workers and urban dwellers, forced to shoulder increasingly high poor rates to provide for improvident immigrants, favored legislation that would shift this burden to Ireland and stem the tide of immigration into England.

In the next chapter we will examine the interpretations of Irish affairs advanced by each of these three schools of thought. Before proceeding it is necessary to touch upon the difficulties inherent in such a presentation. With the exception of the Repeal thesis, which received a formal and coherent articulation, the models of Irish affairs were formulated piecemeal in response to particular Irish questions before the Parliament. The Liberal and Orange models are nowhere codified in a single comprehensive statement. It has therefore been necessary to construct them from the variety of statements and responses made by the British people and government to a series of Irish problems. As a result both models are in fact quite variegated and contain numerous contradictions. For the sake of brevity many of these contradictions have been ignored, and the following presentation is a more internally consistent exposition of the Liberal and Orange models than the sources themselves strictly permit.

Munster and Connaught, poured into Scotland, England and Wales in search of employment. By 1841 the census revealed that 289,404 native-born Irish resided in England and Wales, and 126,321 in Scotland. They formed, respectively, 1.8 percent and 4.8 percent of the total population of those countries. (To these figures must be added the thousands of Irish agricultural laborers who crossed the Irish Sea every year in search of seasonal employment.) The immigrants were not dispersed throughout the country but were heavily concentrated in the "Little Irelands" that grew up in Glasgow, Liverpool, Manchester and London.

Notes

1. See, for example, Elie Halévy, *A History of the English People in the Nineteenth Century,* trans. E. I. Watkin, 6 vols. (New York, 1961); and Llewellyn Woodward, *The Age of Reform: 1815–1870,* 2d ed. rev. (Oxford, 1962).

2. A list of sources is provided in the bibliography. They were drawn from the holdings of the New York Public Library, the British Museum, the Bodleian Library and the library of Trinity College in Dublin.

CHAPTER 4

Images of Ireland—
Shillelaghs and
Smoky Hovels

Poverty

> *The traveler is haunted by the face of popular starvation. It is not the exception, it is the condition of the people. In this fairest and richest of countries, men are suffering and starving by the millions. . . . The epicurean, and traveler for pleasure, had better travel anywhere than here; where there are miseries that one does not dare think of, where one is always feeling how helpless pity is, and how helpless relief, and is perpetually ashamed of being happy.*
>
> WILLIAM THACKERAY

THE REPEAL THESIS

Repealers and their British supporters attributed the poverty of Ireland primarily to the policies of an alien proprietary class. These landlords, many of whom were absentees, were, according to John Stuart Mill, "the very foundation of the economic evils of Ireland." Mill explained that, unlike English

35

proprietors who conceived of their land as an investment and worked to increase its value, Irish landowners viewed their holdings as merely a sinecure that provided them with a yearly revenue.[1] While few of the larger landowners invested their profits in their estates, they nevertheless demanded that the estates return the highest possible rent every year. Repealers argued—with considerable justice according to recent economic historians—that several disastrous consequences emanated from this irresponsible attitude toward the land:

1. *Insecurity of Tenure.* The status of most Irish tenants resembled that of serfs. Rents were not determined by contract but were usually revised at the will of the landlord or his agent. Long-term leases were the general practice only in Ulster. Denied a lease or any guarantee of tenure, a tenant could lawfully be evicted without being reimbursed for any improvements he had made on the land. The landlord could then relet his plot at a higher rent and realize a greater profit. Such a system of tenure was very injurious to the land because it made it advantageous for the tenant to take from the soil without preserving or improving its quality. His economic self-interest dictated that he run down the value of the land to keep his rent from rising.

2. *Subdivision of the Land.* In 1800 the chief export of Ireland was grain, a very profitable crop because the Napoleonic Wars had cut England off from her Continental suppliers. The inflated price of grain encouraged shortsighted landlords to raise their rent and subdivide their land into more numerous smaller plots in order to realize a greater total rent. Given the overpopulation of Ireland the peasantry had no choice but to lease the land on these terms. Two years after the peace treaty the grain market collapsed and most tenants, unable to pay their rent, went into debt. Deprived of their income, numerous landlords went bankrupt and lost their estates. The court-appointed receivers were even more interested in "milking" the land—and the tenantry—in order to realize the cash necessary to repay the former landlord's debts.

3. *Evictions and Conacre.* Landlords in more secure circumstances were sometimes responsible for promoting even greater suffering. After the collapse of the grain market solvent proprietors realized that it was more profitable to convert their estates into dairy farms. Thus some of the best land in Ireland was taken out of cultivation. The peasants evicted from this land were often reduced to begging for a living.

Repealers further noted that Ireland was suffering an industrial decline. The Act of Union, which had removed the trade barriers between Ireland and Britain, worked in practice to the detriment of Irish manufacture by permitting British industrialists, suffering from a depression in the 1820s, to dump their goods on the Irish market. Native industry, unable to compete with the flood of cheap British goods, suffered a grievous decline and the industrial workers, laid off in large numbers, were forced to seek employment in agriculture.

The pressure on the land was further increased by the growing population, which more than doubled between 1800 and 1841. With fewer acres of land in cultivation by reason of the general shift from tillage to grazing, the price of the land became so high that a royal commission estimated that in many counties it actually exceeded the official valuation of the land. The ultimate expression of this struggle for land was the pernicious system of renting known as *conacre*. Under conacre, the tenant let a small plot of land, usually less than three acres, for the duration of one harvest. The owner prepared and manured the soil and the lessee planted his potatoes.* After the harvest the tenant sold his crop in order to pay the rent.

---

*Conacre farming and the entire system of rack-renting, subdivision and short-term leases rested upon the base of potato culture. Contemporary agronomists calculated that the nutritional value of potatoes was higher per acre than that of any cereal grown in Europe. The Victorian scientist Sir Robert Kane estimated that one acre of potatoes could support as much human life as five acres of wheat. Moreover, the potato, unlike cereals, required little capital outlay and was ideally suited to the soil of Ireland.

Conacre rent was so high that unless the peasant harvested a bumper crop he was usually unable to pay. In such cases he was forced to rely upon the charity of his peers for food to last the winter.

Repealers and their British allies proposed a series of measures to strike out at what they perceived to be the root of the evil. Within Parliament they advocated a tax on absentee landlords, lobbied for legislation to govern tenure and protect capital improvement and proposed reform of the encumbrance statutes—laws governing the sale of bankrupt estates. The last of these measures was to facilitate the purchase of land by "improving" landlords who, they hoped, would raise the level of production and improve the general welfare of the people.

The majority of Britons who expressed an opinion on Irish poverty agreed that some legislation was necessary, but they traced the cause of Irish poverty to an altogether different source and advocated reform of quite a different nature.

THE LIBERAL THESIS

By the 1840s enlightened Englishmen were beginning to take a more sociological approach to the problem of poverty. Politicians and economists began to make a distinction between those they believed to have descended into poverty by reason of their personal moral failings and those who were merely prisoners of economic circumstance. Popular novelists like Dickens and Thackeray and leading organs of public opinion, among them *The Times, Edinburgh Review, Punch* and *Blackwood's Magazine,* even suggested that the society had a definite responsibility toward this latter class of poor. Yet the very newspapers, journals and political economists that were sympathetic to the plight of the British lower classes maintained their ancient antipathy toward the paupers of Ireland. The various arguments advanced to demonstrate that poverty at home was as much the result of impersonal economic forces as of personal moral deficiencies were not held to be applicable to Ireland.

The real truth, *The Times* opined, was "that Ireland and the Irish have, in a great measure themselves to thank for their poverty and want of capital. . . . It is by industry, toil, perseverance, economy, prudence, by self-denial, and self-dependence, that a state becomes mighty and its people happy." These were the traits, the newspaper declared, that made England great. Their absence among the Irish of all classes made that country the poorest in Europe. "What is an Englishman made for," *The Times* asked, "but for work? What is an Irishman made for but to sit at his cabin door, read O'Connell's speeches and abuse the English?"[2]

Readers of *The Times* were fed a steady diet of "evidence" in support of this contention by the newspaper's correspondents in Ireland. Their periodic reports portrayed the Irish peasant as ignorant, indolent, scheming and totally irrational and explained the poverty in terms of these characteristics. One such dispatch, dated October 1845, informed the English public:

A more strange mixture than your genuine Irishman it is difficult to conceive. No man will haggle more for 6d., will part with money when he has it with less facility or be more backward to lay out any sum for any useful or profitable object whatever. He is great at a hard bargain, still greater at a job when he supposes he has effectually "done" you. He will take as much pains and resort to as many devices to win 5′ by a job as would win him 50£ by straight forward enterprise. Yet, with all this hardfistedness, he will blindly agree to pay cent. per cent. for the loan of money, which if he *pays* will bring him to ruin.[3]

Fraser's Magazine, popular among the English middle class, echoed these sentiments. One of its contributors declared:

The English people are naturally industrious—they prefer a life of honest labour to one of idleness. They are a persevering as well as energetic race, who for the most part comprehend their own interests perfectly, and sedulously pursue them. Now of all the Celtic tribes, famous everywhere for their indolence and fickleness as the Celts everywhere are, the Irish are admitted to be the most idle and most fickle. They will not work if they can exist without it. Even here in London, though ignorant declaimers assert the reverse, the Irish labourers are the least satisfactory people in the world to deal with.[4]

Punch, radical, satiric and sympathetic to the plight of the British poor, inveighed against the Irish in language that left no doubt about the views of the editors. According to *Punch,* Irishmen were by their very nature the laziest and dirtiest people in all of Europe if not the entire world. Irishmen were "the sons and daughters of generations of beggars. You can trace the descent in their blighted, stunted forms—in their brassy, cunning, brutalized features." Their huts, "Mr. Punch" insisted, were "monuments to national idleness," while the Irish themselves, he theorized, were "the missing link between the gorilla and the Negro."[5]

Chronic self-indulgence, indolence and laxity of purpose were the dominant features of the British image of the Irish which proved useful in explaining the existence of Irish poverty. Other characteristics, such as the Irishmen's proverbial dependence on alcohol, their woeful complacency and their abysmal ignorance and adherence to superstition, were also employed by magazines and parliamentarians to shift the blame for poverty from British to Irish shoulders. It rarely occurred to Englishmen that many of these alleged traits might be the *result,* not the *cause,* of poverty.

Complementing the nearly universal belief that the Irish were morally responsible for their economic inadequacy was the equally prevalent belief that the Irish unlike the English did not mind being poor. This argument was predicated on the assumption that the Irish resembled insensitive animals

more than they did human beings. As far back as the seventeenth century travelers to Ireland returned with the impression that the Irish were racially distinct. One such visitor
wrote:

> In general the outskirts of Dublin consist chiefly of huts, or
> cabbin, constructed of mud dried, and mostly without either
> chimney or window; and in these miserable kind of dwellings, far
> the greater part of the inhabitants of Ireland linger out a
> wretched existence. A small piece of ground is generally an-
> nexed to each, whose chief produce is potatoes; and on these
> roots and milk the common Irish subsist all the year around.
> . . . What little the men can earn by their labour, or the women
> by their spinning, is generally consumed in whiskey. . . . Shoes
> and stockings are seldom worn by these beings *who seem to form
> a different race from the rest of mankind;* their poverty is far greater
> than that of the Spaniards, Portuguese, or even the Scotch peas-
> ants; notwithstanding which, they wear the appearance of con-
> tent.[6]

Many nineteenth-century observers formed a similar impression. A Liverpool physician who undertook to study Irish conditions concluded that "The Irish seem to be as contented
amidst dirt and filth and close confined air, as in clear and airy
situations. While other people would consider comforts, they
appear to have no desire for them; they merely seem to care
for that which will support animal existence."[7]

The Reverend James Page, who toured Ireland in 1836,
made the same observation and warned of the danger of providing relief to the Irish poor:

> The poor Irish work merely for their support; for what can, at
> the lowest calculation, sustain life. That obtained, they sit down
> contentedly in their cabins, in the midst of filth and wretched-
> ness almost exceeding what the greatest stretch of an English-
> man's imagination can conceive. For subsistence they will work,
> and that with cheerfulness. Beyond this their degraded condi-
> tion does not permit them to pass. To hold out to such people

a prospect of support . . . might prove injurious in the highest degree.[8]

Another contemporary observed:

> In an intercourse with the common people, a day, an hour, cannot pass without being struck by some mark of talent, some display of an imagination at once glowing and enthusiastic, or some touch of tender and delicate feeling. How strange it is, that such a people should be content to dwell in smoky hovels, when, if they chose to exert themselves and employ their energies which I think they possess, their conditions might be improved. But they are generally happy; therefore why wish to alter their state?[9]

This argument was commonplace in leading British newspapers and magazines. *Fraser's Magazine,* for example, lamented the fact that Irishmen were content to live amidst poverty even after they had been exposed to the better things in life by emigration to Britain. Even more reprehensible, it commented, was the Irish tendency to do violence to anyone who was industrious and improved his fortune. *Fraser's* concluded that it was England's duty to effect a "moral revolution" in Ireland.[10]

The Times informed its readers that Irish poverty had to be understood within the Irish context. Was it Britain's fault if the Irish preferred potatoes to bread and chose to live in conditions that even their pigs would not tolerate? In the opinion of the editors, "The uncivilized habits of the Irish have made them callous to so much of their poverty as does not *press* upon them in the shape of actual hunger, and have therefore tended to perpetuate that poverty through successive generations."[11]

A representative of more conservative opinion, *Blackwood's Magazine,* went even further in differentiating the Irish from the English. Its Irish correspondent reported: "The people are fond of coarse food, which we think unfit for men, but they prefer it . . . the Irish consider the use of 'bread and meat', as an infliction." Blind to the real ills of Ireland, *Blackwood's*

pushed this argument to its logical conclusion: "The truth is
. . . that though there is more squalid filth and raggedness in
Ireland (for those are national tastes) there is much less real
misery or distress in that country than exists in England."[12]

Poverty, therefore, had a relative not an absolute meaning. The poor and unemployed in Britain were to be pitied
because they were largely prisoners of circumstance who suffered their deprivation quietly and aspired to improve their
lot. The Irish on the other hand enjoyed their degradation—
or at least did not object strenuously—and would continue to
remain impoverished as a result. With this distinction in mind,
parliamentarians reasoned that, although Ireland was statisti-
cally more depressed than Britain, the government and private
charities ought to be more concerned with alleviating British
distress.[13]

Violence

*The very name [Ireland] forces to our recollection images of
shillelaghs, and broken heads, and turbulence of every kind.*

HENRY INGLIS

Another salient feature of the Irish problem was the frequent
outbreak of both spontaneous violence and organized terror-
ism in the Irish countryside. For most British observers, violence, like poverty, had one meaning in England and quite
another in Ireland.

Repealers argued that agrarian violence in Ireland, like
urban disorder in England, was a response to the severe economic distress of the lower classes. Deprived of a lease, subject
to sudden eviction from the land and denied any effective
relief by the state, the Irish peasant resorted to violence as his
last weapon against the policies of the landlords. According to
Repealers, the peasants' violence was directed only against

landlords and estate agents—both Catholic and Protestant—
who were responsible for rack-renting and mass evictions.
Sharman Crawford, one of the more responsible Protestant
landowners in Ireland, testified to the selectivity of peasant
violence. Speaking out against an arms bill sponsored by the
Peel ministry, he warned his fellow parliamentarians that

> It was the system of oppression by Irish landlords which caused
> the disposition among the people to agrarian outrage. They
> could get no justice from the law, and they were compelled to
> make a law for themselves; and that said, we must protect our-
> selves or starve. The way to remedy the existing evils was by
> improving the condition of the people.[14]

Within Britain, this view was endorsed by some noted
economists, among them George Poulett Scrope, John Pitt
Kennedy and John Stuart Mill. In a pamphlet first published
in 1834, Scrope urged the government to curb the nearly
absolute power of the landlords. Without such reform, he
warned, Britain would be faced with a starving peasantry and
the likelihood of revolution in Ireland:

> It is impossible . . . to have any doubt as to the real cause of the
> insurrectionary spirit and agrarian outrages of the Irish peas-
> antry. They are the struggles of an oppressed starving people for
> existence! They are the rude efforts at obtaining a sort of savage
> self-established justice. . . . They are the natural and necessary
> results of a state of law which allows the landlords of a country
> at one time to encourage an excessive growth of population on
> their estates, and at another, when caprice seizes them, to dis-
> possess all this population, and turn them out on the highways
> without food and shelter.[15]

Yet despite the cogent analysis of British economists, the
agitation of the radical press and the evidence submitted by
government commissions, most Englishmen refused to admit
the connection between distress and violence in Ireland. Having already minimized the extent of poverty in Ireland, they

preferred to explain "outrages" in terms of the Irish proclivity for disruption.

At the turn of the nineteenth century, the image of the violent Irishman was endemic to popular novels, plays and amusing stories circulated by word of mouth. One such anecdote, related by John Carr, is indicative of the general characterization of the Celt as violent but amusing. An Irishman, suddenly the recipient of a large fortune, embarked upon a grand tour of the Continent.

> After passing through France and Italy, and part of Spain, with scarcely any emotions of delight, he entered a village in the latter country where he saw a mob fighting very desperately, upon which in a moment he sprang out of his travelling carriage without once inquiring into the cause of the battle, or ascertaining which side he ought in justice to espouse, he laid about him with his shilala, and after having had several of his teeth knocked out, and an eye closed, and the bridge of his nose broken, he returned to his carriage, and exclaimed, "By Jasus! it is the only bit of fun I have had since I left Ireland."[16]

Carr's Irishman was the "stage Irishman," a stock character in English comedies from the days of Shakespeare. For centuries his antics had amused English audiences and helped to perpetuate the stereotype. In Victorian times, this playful ridicule of "Paddy" found its epitome in the caricatures of Irishmen that filled the pages of *Punch.*

Mr. Punch was shocked by the "howls of indignant and disruptive Irishmen." He considered those who raised their voices—or shillelaghs—in protest to be uncouth, as no Englishman would be, and as only the Irish could be, although Americans ran a close second. Irish violence, according to *Punch,* was not a result of grievances but merely a reflection of the turbulent character of the people. Their "chief delight," Mr. Punch observed, "seems to consist in getting into all manner of scrapes, for the mere purpose of displaying their ingenuity by getting out of them again." This could be observed in every aspect of their behavior: Irish politicians were "natives of Ireland, who are always quarreling with each other, and everyone else." "Moral force," O'Connell's means of appeal to English hearts, consisted of "Brick-bats, fruit in an advanced state of decomposition, blazing tar barrels, and shillelaghs." Irish tribunals were composed of "accuser and accused—placed twelve paces apart to prevent accidents—a couple of judges and a surgeon."[17]

This image began to darken in response to the rising incidence of outrages in Ireland. By 1840 a more vicious image of Irishmen, in which humor was noticeably lacking, had begun to dominate British perceptions. Returning travelers portrayed the Irish as the most savage, most desperate and most uncivilized people on the face of the earth. The Irish, one such visitor exclaimed, "would rather gain possession by their blood than by their labour."[18] "The murders of this country," declared another, "would disgrace the most gloomy wilds of the most savage tribes that ever roamed in Asia, Africa, or America."[19] The British public learned of the Irish that "Their very amusements are polemical: fighting is a pastime which they seldom assemble without enjoying. . . . When not driven by necessity, they willingly consume whole days in sloth, or as willingly employ them in riot; strange diversity of nature to love indolence and hate quiet—to be reduced to slavery, but not yet to obedience."[20] Still another traveler was convinced that their "turbulent spirit is so averse to order and peace that no prince or legislator their country ever produced was able to control them."[21]

The extent to which this image became dogma in the 1840s is reflected in the multitude of characterizations of perverse and violent Irishmen found in the leading organs of public opinion. Among the major British newspapers and journals analyzed in this study, only the *Morning Chronicle*, the *Westminster Review* and the *Northern Star*—the last a spokesman for radical opinion—rejected this caricature of the Irish peasant. *Fraser's Magazine*, *Blackwood's Magazine*, *Punch*, *The Times*, the *Illustrated London News* and the several Peelite papers all

THE IRISH FRANKENSTEIN.

The monster Repeal attacks a respectable England. From *Punch* (1843).

subscribed to the belief that the refractory nature of the Celt led him to take up arms against life and property. They vociferously denied the contention of the Repealers that violence was connected with the mismanagement of Irish land.

The Times, truly representative of British opinion in this respect, heaped continual derision upon the Celtic character, which it assured its readers was the real cause of outrages in Ireland. In December 1845 the newspaper declared that "The Irish have no feeling for law and order. If someone is killed or injured their sympathies are for the perpetrator of the deed and not the one who suffers. And if the deed should be proved and punished, they howl as if an innocent man had been convicted."[22]

The editors, shocked by the barbarities committed by other nations and peoples, could usually discern some method to their madness. With respect to Ireland they confessed their utter confusion. The violent outbursts of that country were so frequent and so obviously uninspired by any real grievances that they defied explanation. In October 1846 the newspaper concluded that

> An Irishman commits a murder as a Malay runs a-muck. In certain circumstances it is expected of him, and he would be thought a mean and spiritless wretch if he demurred at it. It is only unfortunate that these circumstances are so indefinite. The conditions under which a Malay draws his krise for the last rush, like those which dictate self-immolation in Japan, are pretty well known by all persons conversant with the native character, and precautions can sometimes be taken against the catastrophe. Even in MADRID and VENICE, the insults to be washed out only by blood were defined with some precision. But it is impossible to catalogue the offenses which amongst Irishmen entail sudden murder or secret assassination.[23]

Peelite and Liberal politicians subscribed, both publicly and privately, to the views expressed by *The Times*. Robert Peel, nicknamed "Orange Peel" by the Irish, was particularly shocked by the prevalence of violence in Ireland and his gov-

ernment's failure to put an end to it. Attributing the difficulty
to the unwillingness of Irishmen to testify against suspected
murderers, he related his exasperation to James Graham, the
home secretary:

> There seems a general impression in Ireland that nothing will
> effect this [testimony against murderers] but a pecuniary motive,
> that the people are so radically corrupt and sanguinary that
> there is a sympathy with the Murderer—and that selfishness and
> the fear of pecuniary [loss] must supply the motives to give
> evidence against an Assassin which the natural and intuitive
> feelings of mankind supply in more favored Countries.[24]

Graham held an equally derogatory view of the Irish character and agreed with Peel that the moral depravity of Ireland
was unique in Europe.[25] Lord Eliot, chief secretary for Ireland
in Peel's second ministry, echoed these sentiments. Speaking
for the government in support of an arms bill, Eliot justified
the measure by reason of the "thirst for arms" which he
thought "a ruling passion among so many peasantry." He
informed the Parliament that "There is, I regret to say, an
unhappy propensity among the Irish peasantry to effect their
ends, whatever those ends be, by intimidation and violence."[26]

The Whigs opposed the arms bills of the Tories for political reasons but nevertheless subscribed to basically the same
view of Irish affairs. The public pronouncements of Lord John
Russell, leader of the Opposition during Peel's second ministry, were largely indistinguishable from those of his political
rival. In 1836 Russell told an audience in Bristol: "You all
know, indeed, it has now become a matter of too frequent
occurrence for any one to be ignorant of the fact, that in
Ireland there prevail crimes among the peasantry . . . crimes
too often of confederacy and combination." Was the origin of
such violence to be traced to the just grievances of the Irish?
No, Russell replied, it lay in the character of the people. "What
do we want in that country? With regard to this *moral complaint,*
this perverted sense of what is right and what is wrong, we

want the means to teach the great principles of religion and morality."[27] Accordingly Russell, who came to power in 1846 by defeating an arms bill of Robert Peel, proposed and carried his own arms bill in 1847.

Russell's bill appealed to both the leadership and the rank and file of his party. Charles Greville, the renowned diarist, the Earl of Clarendon, lord lieutenant of Ireland, Charles Wood, the home secretary, and Thomas Macaulay, the famous historian and reformer, all spoke of the need to carry out a moral reformation in Ireland. Macaulay, an influential proponent of the first Reform Act, was instrumental in popularizing an interpretation of Irish history based upon the Celtic love of violence and anarchy. In his widely read *History of England* he explained the periodic rebellions of the Irish as a function of their degraded character. With respect to the uprising of 1690, he explained, "The habits of the Celtic peasant were such that he made no sacrifice in quitting his potato ground for the camp. He loved excitement and adventure. He feared work more than danger. . . . Far more seductive bait than his miserable stipend was the promise of boundless license."[28]

Repeal Agitation

> Daniel O'Connell 'd no mischief to brew
> So he started Repeal just for something to do.
> And the watch-word like mad through Hibernia ran;
> "Och! the rent is a mighty fine income," says Dan.
>
> PUNCH

THE LIBERAL THESIS

If poverty, violence and the generally depressed state of Ireland were, as the British declared, manifestations of moral deficiencies in the Celtic character, and not the result of British misrule, the government and people could hardly admit to the legitimacy of the Repeal movement. Thus it is not surprising to find that the goal of Repeal was dismissed as impractical, the means through which it was advanced denounced as self-defeating and its proponents derided as self-seeking agitators.

British organs of public opinion, the broadside and pamphlet literature and the statements of leading political figures abounded in virulent invective directed against Daniel O'Connell. The fury of these attacks rose in proportion to the success of the Repeal movement in Ireland. In the middle eighteen-forties, when O'Connell had rallied the Irish masses behind the banner of Repeal, the fury of charge and countercharge rose to such a frenzied pitch that contemporary wags quipped that the format of the British press would soon have to be expanded if other news was to be reported.

Most Englishmen believed O'Connell to be self-seeking, unscrupulous and insincere. In both the press and pamphlet literature he was portrayed as coldly calculating, shrewd—even brilliant—and intent on increasing his own power at the expense of both the Irish people and the British government. The noted economist Nassau Senior expressed the general consensus when he declared: "We do not reckon Mr. O'Connell among the sincere Repealers. He knows too much to believe that Repeal can be obtained by force; and he has too much to lose to desire a sanguinary contest." Senior lamented the fact that "unfortunately for himself and his country, all his angry and all his selfish passions appear to drive him to manifest the same feelings."[29]

If, as Senior believed, O'Connell merely manipulated the Repeal movement in support of his personal ambitions, it was reasonable to conclude that the government could gain nothing by attempting to satisfy the demands of the Repealers; they would simply invent new issues in order to continue the agitation. Accordingly Senior warned against concessions. The newspapers and publicists of the day reflected the predominance of this point of view. The Reverend James Page warned: "Grant these men what they ask from time to time, and still they will find some new grievances, so long as they can derive a much better income from agitation than they could possibly earn in an honest way."[30] *The Times*, drawing the argument to its logical conclusion, suggested that eventually the Repealers would object to the very existence of the British nation: "We really expect soon to be told that it is a grievance and an insult to Ireland even to look at an Irishman, or to talk of him, or to walk with him, or to do him a service. These gentlemen [the Repealers] are like the querulous old man in the fable—do what you will you can't please them."[31]

The tempestuous character of Irish politics, the oratory and display of Repeal and the particularly colorful but enigmatic personality of O'Connell provided the ammunition for a second image of the Liberator, as he was called: that of the clown and mountebank, clever but not astute, powerful but ludicrous, and more dedicated to extravagance, display and nuisance than to the aggrandizement of his power. *Punch*, as might be expected, was the leading proponent of this view. In the pages of that magazine, the Liberator and his coterie of followers were subjected to incessant scathing satire.

In 1843 *Punch* described the "O'Connell Statue," a supposed monument to be erected in Dublin by his faithful supporters. O'Connell was to be depicted astride three men dressed in the tattered remnants of clothes. One would hold a harp, while another was blindfolded by a rag upon which "Repeal" was inscribed. The dedication would read: "To Daniel O'Connell, who has identified the interests of his countrymen with his own, by endeavouring to make his own whatever belongs to them." On another occasion *Punch* reported that an Irish-American had bequeathed five hundred dollars to O'Connell. Mr. Punch asked: "Is there no way to make him forego repeal, bound as he is to it by five hundred dollars? Yes; one way there is. Offer him SIX!" Nevertheless, the magazine felt compelled to admit that O'Connell was a fair representative of Hibernia: "For seeing the great Liberator, the imagination immediately conjures up a lyre."[32]

The newspapers were not nearly so playful in their treatment of O'Connell. The *Illustrated London News*, the *Herald*, the

Standard and the *Morning Post* lashed out at O'Connell's deceit and the disruptive effect of his agitation upon Ireland. *The Times* was particularly acrimonious. John Walter II, the owner, loathed O'Connell, his political program and his religion and allowed his newspaper to carry the most libelous denunciations of him.[33] In one article alone *The Times* described O'Connell as "scum condensed of Irish bog," "a greedy self-serving satan," a man "whose principles we hold in abhorrence, as those of the worst being in human form that ever disgraced the floor of an English Senate."[34] Each success of Repeal was analyzed only in terms of how it personally enriched the Liberator because, the newspaper reasoned, the hoax of Repeal was so obvious that Repealers must be either very deluded people or self-seeking despots. At least one historian sees *The Times'* repetitive and strident opposition as having robbed O'Connell of much of the sympathy he might otherwise have received from the English public.[35]

Within Parliament the Tories upheld the sentiment of *The Times*. They attacked Repeal as a delusion designed to enrich O'Connell and his cabal at the expense of the impoverished peasantry. The following extract from the report of one speech is illustrative of their abusive diatribes against O'Connell.

> He [the speaker] would refer the House to one who had made money in Ireland not as the inculcator of Christian truth, but as the minister of sedition. He could refer them to one whose exertions in that character had done more to feed the gibbet and to fill the convict ship than all the other causes that were active in that unhappy country. Nor were such exertions gratuitous; for the penury of the poor, who had been dupes of his delusions, was taxed to remunerate his services, and the tribute, as it was called, had been in many cases extorted under the threat of ecclesiastical anathemas in Ireland.[36]

The Tory leadership—Robert Peel, the Duke of Wellington and James Graham—agreed with these sentiments, al-

KING O'CONNELL AT TARA.

A view of O'Connell and his followers. From *Punch* (1843).

though they expressed themselves in a less hysterical tone. They were convinced that O'Connell could put an end to agrarian violence in Ireland if he wished to do so and that he chose instead to encourage it in order to advance his own political fortunes. They were shocked that the Whigs could make a political alliance with such a man. After the Litchfield Compact between O'Connell and the Whigs in 1835, the Duke of Wellington wrote to Peel that the Irish government would now consist of "Folly and Vanity mutually offering incense to each other, & kneeling together in joint adoration at the bloody shrine of O'Connell."[37]

Robert Peel bore a special animosity toward O'Connell that dated back to the early years of the century when Peel had served as undersecretary for Ireland. By the 1830s the feud between the two men had reached such proportions that they agreed to settle it by a duel. The affair was prevented at the last minute when the government, informed of it by O'Connell's wife, forbade Peel to endanger his life.[38] In many ways the conflict between the British government and the Repeal Association was personified in the struggle between these two strong-willed men.

The Whigs at first viewed O'Connell in a more favorable light than did the Tories. They supported Catholic emancipation in 1828–1829 and in 1835 entered into their parliamentary alliance with O'Connell. In 1840, however, O'Connell, who objected to the extremely cautious nature of Whig reform, broke the alliance and the honeymoon ended. In 1837 Charles Greville had described O'Connell as "all moderation," a man whose influence was carefully directed to the goal of reform in Ireland. In 1840, after O'Connell had returned to the idea of Repeal, Greville sang a different tune. Now he declared the Liberator to be a "moral deformity," although he remained convinced that O'Connell had no wish to provoke revolution in Ireland.[39] Lord Clarendon evidenced a similar change of mind. In the early forties, at the height of the Repeal agitation, he wrote to a friend: "If he [O'Connell] had ceased agitating when emancipation was carried, he would have been as great a man in his way as Washington; but he continued it for purposes most mischievous as regards the people and most selfish as regards himself. His whole object was money and power; that latter in order to make it subservient to the former."[40]

The idea of O'Connell's inherent bad faith, subscribed to by leading Whigs, is well illustrated by an incident that took place in December 1839. The Whig administration, eager to settle with O'Connell, authorized the Marquess of Anglesey to offer him the mastership of the Irish Rolls. Should the Liberator decline the proposal he was to be offered the chief justiceship of Calcutta. O'Connell indignantly rejected both sinecures, telling Anglesey that he could be "bought" only by meaningful Irish reform. The Marquess concluded only that O'Connell was holding out for a more lucrative position. He reported to Melbourne, the prime minister, that O'Connell "is *not to be had.* He is flying at higher game than a judgeship, and he is secure of a better income from the deluded people than *any Government* can venture to give *any Person* whatever."[41]

Despite the nearly universal British belief that O'Connell was a charlatan and that Repeal was a hoax, the stubborn fact remained that the Repeal movement prospered in Ireland; the Irish masses were willing to advance the cause with their voices, their money and—the British feared—their shillelaghs. If Repeal was really the plot of agitators, why did the Irish people support it so enthusiastically and welcome it as their hope for salvation? If the grievances articulated by the agitators were imaginary and their proposed panacea absurd, why did the masses flock to Repeal meetings, contribute funds they could ill afford and deliver their votes to Repealers at the polls?

Once again, Englishmen drew upon the panoply of national characteristics they attributed to Irishmen to explain away this disturbing phenomenon. *Punch* explained that the strength of Repeal rested on the ignorance and naiveté of the Irish people. "Mr. O'Connell knows too well," *Punch* declared, "it is only by keeping an Irishman's head in ignorance of what his hand and heart are led to do, that, when he sends round the hat, he can make sure of his shilling." The success of this tactic, according to *Punch*, was well illustrated by an incident concerning a six-year-old lad's contribution to Repeal. Upon offering his Repeal rent to the Repeal warden, young Tim Doolan was overheard to say: "Here's sixpence an English gentleman gav'd me for holding his horse in Phaynix [Phoenix Park, Dublin]. Say it's from an inimy of the Saxon." Ignorant of their true benefactor, *Punch* reasoned, young Tim Doolan and other Irishmen knew no better than to bite the hand that fed them. The magazine could express pity for these "good-natured simple Paddies, who roar at all your [O'Connell's] jokes, hurray at all your lies, come leagues upon leagues to attend your show, and have paid their money so often."[42]

The Times voiced similar sentiments, tracing the success of Repeal to the childlike nature of the Celt, so cleverly manipulated by O'Connell to serve his own ends. In January 1843, for example, the newspaper declared:

> A people of acute sensibilities and lively passions, more quick in feeling wrongs than rational in explaining or temperate in addressing them—as easily roused into outrage by supposed oppression as subdued into docility by felicitous kindness—equally susceptible of gratitude for hypocritical sympathy as of indignation at unintentional or imaginary injury—no less impetuous in repaying the one than ardent in avenging the other—such is the people whose virtues and whose vices . . . O'Connell has so fiendishly exploited.[43]

Supporting Repeal was like grasping at straws, yet the Irish people fell for O'Connell's lies and helped him to achieve his ambition. Now all that was to be heard in Ireland, *The Times* warned the public in June 1843, was a "vague indefinite notion of wide-spread, loud-tongued, but not very accountable discontent. . . . All is inconsistency, contradiction, passion, and exaggeration."[44] The only hope for Ireland, *The Times* concluded, was that its wiser men might not be swayed by agitators or duped like the simple ignorant peasants into "a suicidal divorce" with England.[45]

THE ORANGE THESIS

Most of the British political elite, while horrified by the thought of Repeal, accepted the need for some reform in Ireland, as was evidenced by the passage, for example, of the Irish Poor Law and the Encumbered Estates Act. In contrast, the spokesmen of the Anglo-Protestant ruling class in Ireland denied *any* cause for Irish Catholic grievances. To their reckoning, "the Irish people ought to feel not only content, but *grateful* for the situation they were placed in."[46] They maintained that the peasantry were carefree and content and that only those who were misled by the agitators expressed dissatisfaction with the existing state of affairs. Like plantation owners in the antebellum American South, the majority of Irish landowners insisted that they alone comprehended the peasant's needs and acted on his behalf. The agitators, who sought to disrupt this "natural" relationship, must be crushed.

Ascendancy spokesmen consistently hammered away at the theme that the Irish peasant, ignorant, superstitious and easily led astray, was seduced by the false promises of Repeal to partake in the agitation, the real effect of which he did not comprehend. One Irish Tory informed the House of Commons that

> He believed the mass of the Irish people who clamoured for Repeal knew not what they asked for. The Russian mob once clamoured for the Constitution, and when asked what it meant, said the Constitution was the wife of Constantine. The Russian peasants were philosophers to the Irish. . . .[47]

Most Irish Whigs echoed these sentiments. In 1843 Frederick Shaw told the House that, "As to Repeal of the Union, it was a mere delusion. In Ireland no one was duped by it, except the unfortunate beings who were collected by masses in its name." Should Repeal ever come to pass, Shaw insisted, the Irish would "be released from all obligations of civilised society." *The Times,* it is interesting to note, quoted these and other parts of Shaw's speech in support of its own condemnation of Repeal.[48]

When challenged to explain O'Connell's appeal to the masses, Ascendancy spokesmen traced his success to the proverbial Irish love of display and oratory. The Liberator, they explained, cleverly played upon the Irishmen's love of fiery declarations and appealed to both their romantic nature and their vanity. One anonymous pamphleteer declared: "The cry for Repeal of the Union *became* the *compendious expression* of the collective grievances and *wants* of the people, and one could hardly have been selected more catching to Irish ears. It first of all flattered the national vanity and fed that taste for romance and mystification which everyone knows is inherent in the Irish peasantry."[49] An Irish minister described Repeal as essentially an amusement:

> Yes, as great a boon as emancipation was, [it was] no sooner granted than a new puppet is up for the amusement and deception of the spectators, and to the no small advantage of the showmen. The fact is, that the Irish people care as little about these matters, as we can conceive. I know that they may be congregated as an anti-tithe meeting, to denounce that "incubus," the established church, the greater part of them, not knowing wherefore they are called together. . . . Irish people! poor creatures, knowing them as I do, it is quite amusing to hear them thus dignified by being supposed to take an interest in the stormy discussions in the House of Commons.[50]

The Marquess of Westmeath, a leading Ascendancy spokesman, contended that the peasantry had taken no interest in political questions until aroused by the agitators. Even then, he asserted, the peasantry were content and failed to realize how such agitation endangered their welfare. In 1846 the Marquess expounded this theory to the House of Lords:

> As to the assertions . . . of extreme discontent of the Irish with the Imperial Government, he [the Marquess] denies its existence. The people of Ireland had in their hearts no such feeling. The Repeal agitation and other agitation which had been going on for a length of time, had done all that industry and perseverance and talent could do to alienate the feelings of the Irish people from the country.[51]

As an Irish representative peer, the Marquess felt that it was his duty to assert that the Irish people were not discontented. What ill feeling did exist, he insisted, was manufactured by the Irish press for the purpose of sedition. The press "was maintained by large sums of money, and circulated gratis, and it lost no opportunity of exasperating the people against the Saxon; but the heart of the Irish people was sound."[52]

While the majority of Englishmen believed that Repeal was motivated by the pecuniary greed of the agitators, most Orange spokesmen saw in it something infinitely more threatening; they discerned the long arm of Rome behind every move of O'Connell and every act of murder and assassination. Irish Tories declared that "Repeal is just a discreet word for Romish ascendancy and *Protestant extermination.* So far from there being a cessation of Romish aggression, or desire for supremacy, it is more marked, decided, and uncompromising than at any former period in the history of the country."[53]

In reality, Repeal was far from being a Catholic plot, even though it was supported by the majority of parish priests in Ireland. The church hierarchy feared Repeal more than they abhorred the Protestant Ascendancy and the established church. The bishops disliked the democratic structure of the movement and suspected O'Connell of harboring thoughts of radical social and economic reform. They perceived Repeal as a threat to both the social order and the precarious position of the Catholic church. The pope was even more opposed to Repeal; during the height of O'Connell's agitation the Vatican entered into negotiations with Robert Peel and appeared ready to speak out against the agitation in return for concessions to the church by the government.[54] Nevertheless, the Tory landlords, frightened by the political and economic goals of the movement, played upon the religious question in the hope of mobilizing popular support in Britain.

The Marquess of Westmeath characterized the Irish priests as "relentless and intriguing . . . men whose conduct at all times proved they were inimical to civil liberty. The history of all times in which popery existed," he told the House of Lords, "fully bore him out in attributing to them those qualities."[55] The Earl of Winchelsea declared: "The whole mass of the Roman Catholic population of Ireland, and nearly the whole hierarchy of that country united with the avowed object of the destruction of the Church [of Ireland]."[56] The Earl of Roden, one of the most outspoken Irish peers on the subject of Repeal, urged the government to crush the agitation and save the Protestant faith in Ireland. "It has been openly and distinctly stated," he informed his fellow peers, "that the destruction of the Protestant religion was one of the objects of Repealers."[57]

Across the Irish Sea the appeals of the Irish Tories found a receptive audience in the country squires who formed the right wing of the Tory party. Young Benjamin Disraeli, aspiring to capture the leadership of this faction, articulated their sentiments toward Ireland in a series of articles that appeared in *The Times* in 1836. Disraeli charged that the Irish "hate our free and fertile isle. They hate our order, our civilisation, our enterprising industry, our sustained courage, our decorous liberty, our pure religion. This wild, reckless, indolent, uncertain, and superstitious race has no sympathy with the English character." The Irish, he exclaimed, stood for the very antithesis of the character traits admired in England. "Their fair idea of human felicity is an alternation of damnish broils and coarse idolatry. Their history described an unbroken circle of bigotry and blood. My Lords," he asked parenthetically, "shall the delegates of these tribes, under the direction of the Roman priesthood, ride roughshod over our country—over England —haughty and still imperial England?"[58]

Disraeli reserved his most abusive invective for O'Connell, who he claimed was "a systematic liar and a beggarly cheat, a swindler and a poltroon," whose "public life and private life are equally profligate; he has committed every crime that does not require courage."[59] The Tory squires were delighted. O'Connell was outraged, of course, and challenged Disraeli to a duel.

Disraeli's articles also found a sympathetic audience among substantial numbers of middle-class Englishmen for whom the Catholic church was still the archenemy of the British nation. *Blackwood's Magazine,* which gave expression to this segment of opinion, described O'Connell's leadership as "a reign of terror—of moral terror, if you will—but of terror quite as effectual, and more powerful than that of the guillotine, a terror which pervades all classes of society, which is 'exercised by persons unseen, and for causes unknown.' "[60] It condemned Repeal as "Rampant mendicancy . . . its mouth full of grievances and its bag full of priest pence." The magazine warned that "Ireland and Rome are as powerful objects of anxiety as in the days of Pius and Elizabeth and Protestantism is forced to be as vigilant as in the days when . . . the Long Parliament drove the bishops out of the Pale of the Constitution."[61] As proof of this assertion, *Blackwood's* referred to numbers of parliamentarians who, it insisted, were in the pay of the church.[62]

Protestant pamphleteers elaborated upon this thesis and sought to explain the power of the church. Most frequently, they attributed it to the "pernicious" doctrine of confession, by which the clergy absolved the peasantry of their sins. One representative pamphleteer penned the following lines:

> How dreary Britain's prospect from the hour
> When such deluded men advanced to power!
> No wonder of incendiaries we read!
> *Twelve shillings* will atone for such a deed!!!
> For *ten and sixpence* every Priest may do
> What Protestants are taught with scorn to view.
> For *four pounds odd* the Papist may apply
> The murderer's knife!!! a father to destroy!!![63]

The priesthood was usually described as the drill sergeant of Repeal. Allied with Repealers and radicals, they urged their parishioners to murder landlords and opposition candidates, according to the Orange penmen. The literature painted a frightening picture of the priests at the altar, inciting their congregations to commit all kinds of bestial crimes against the Protestants who barred their way to power. One pamphleteer provided this description:

> They stand at the altar, these dark ministers of a dark faith, arrayed in the mysterious power which their imagined authority over the next world gives them, and with the substantial power which they derive from their influence in this. When they speak, every voice is still; where they point the finger, the eyes of all follow it; and from the altar, inflamed by bigotry and delighting in blood, rush out the savage populace, to seize upon the victim, and to consign to destruction his property, his family, his home, and his life. Blood is the order—Blood is the cry—Blood is the doom![64]

Opposing Remedies

Ye English, a rush for your conciliation!
Alike your persuasion and force we defy;
We detest, we abominate you as a nation,
We hate you the worse the more kindness you try.

PUNCH

The preceding analysis suggests that the British elite and the Repealers held opposite images of the truth. The Repeal idea of cause and effect, which attributed Ireland's poverty and violence to centuries of British domination, was completely reversed in the British analysis of Irish affairs.

Proponents of both the Orange and Liberal models of the Irish problem took a stereotyped image of Irishmen as their a priori assumption. This stereotype, depicted in the preceding pages, portrayed the Irish as cunning but ignorant, cowardly but brazenly rash, religious and superstitious, indolent, complacent and addicted to both violence and alcohol. These characteristics provided the basis for arguments dismissing the contentions of Repealers.

The British declared that the Irish remained poor because they were too lazy to work and too self-complacent to be bothered by their poverty. They were violent because they loved disruption more than peace and were too ignorant to see the consequences of continuous turbulence. They supported political agitation because they were superstitious and misled by the Catholic church or because they were rash and undiscerning and misled by the pomp and oratory of Repealers. Repeal had thus gained an ascendancy over the Irish that no similar movement ever could achieve over the British.

The Repeal movement itself, according to most British commentators, only aggravated the condition of Ireland by promoting outrages, thus discouraging Irish landlords and British capitalists from investing their wealth in that country. As a result, the growing population became still more impoverished and more open to the appeal of the agitators. In this way the Repeal agitators had created a vicious cycle of outrage and reaction that was slowly destroying Ireland.

Given the divergent diagnoses of Ireland's ills expounded by the Irish "agitators" and the British observers, it was inevitable that the two groups would prescribe different courses of treatment for those ills. For Repealers the cure lay with economic reform and the admission of Ireland into the pale of the British Constitution. For the British commentators—and the majority of the British people—the downward spiral of distress and reaction could be halted only by the repression of violence and a corresponding reformation of the Irish people. Only *after* tranquility was restored to Ireland, the British reasoned, could the government carry out reforms conducive to the economic development of that unhappy island. This argument provided the rationale for the Peel administration's response to the agitation—the dismissal of Repealers from public office, the arrest and trial of Repeal leaders as conspirators and the repression of the Repeal press. It also provided the justification for one of the major legislative responses to the Repeal challenge—the Arms Act of 1843, a police measure designed to extend the licensing of arms and the punishment of persons illegally in possession of them.

This measure was very popular among the British people. With the exception of the *Morning Chronicle*, the *Westminster Review* and the radical *Northern Star*, all the organs of English public opinion analyzed in this study voiced the popular desire for coercion first and concession afterwards. In January 1843 the editors of *Freeman's Journal*, an independent Irish newspaper with Repeal sympathies, expressed the following complaint:

> The cry is now for strong measures. Such is the language which is now held by the English journals, which, in their habitual ignorance and presumption, undertake to supply remedies for a social condition, with whose disturbing elements they are utterly unacquainted. They argue from facts of their own creation,

and presuppose a state of things to give colour to their absurdities.[65]

Blackwood's Magazine was one of those journals to which the editors referred. Tory in sympathies, *Blackwood's* endorsed Peel's policy, reasoning that repressive measures had to be carried out "in mercy to the peasantry themselves." The magazine described such a policy as both the wisest and most humane course the government could follow:

> There is a remedy for the ills of Ireland, and a simple and efficacious remedy it will be found to be, if adopted. Enforce obedience to the laws, establish security of life and property, no matter at what sacrifice or by what means. The more severe and uncompromising the measures by which those objects shall be sought to be effectuated, the more prompt will be the success, and the more merciful the operation.[66]

In June 1843 *The Times* exclaimed: "The moving principle of the assemblies [of Repeal] . . . is hostility to 'the Saxon'— and the indefinite desire for an imaginary independence." The newspaper reluctantly concluded that such a country must be ruled with an iron hand. In September *The Times* declared that England had until now followed the wrong policy toward Ireland. The government had made concession after concession in hope of attaining peace when it "should coerce first, get Ireland securely in hand, *then* make concessions to her needs."[67]

Fraser's Magazine reasoned that Ireland "must continue to be the great difficulty of every minister of the British Crown till there shall arise a man possessed of nerve and influence enough to deal with that land of anomalies as it deserves." The magazine warned:

> Ireland is not ripe for the blessings of the free constitution which has been forced upon it before the time, and which its people do not know how to use. We have been striving for these last thirty years and more to conciliate, when we ought all the while to have been governing with the strong hand. . . .[68]

Repealers, exasperated by the popular clamor for repressive legislation, declared that such a policy violated the very premise upon which the Union was based. How could Englishmen who claimed to govern Ireland in the same spirit with which they governed Britain respond differently to similar problems in both countries? Outrage in England was not met with arms bills, suspension of civil liberties and the declaration of martial law; the British people would not stand for it. Here was the very circumstance that justified demands for repeal of the Union. British parliamentarians refused to accept the validity of the analogy, responding that constitutional principles were relative, not absolute, and must be molded to the character and moral development of the people to which they were applied; with respect to Ireland and England coercion was justified in the one case but not in the other. Expanding upon this argument, *The Times* declared:

> To Englishmen a vigour beyond the Constitution is an odious thing. The powers granted by the Constitution they have always found adequate to meet emergency and danger. And it seems unkind and unjust to recommend for Irishmen a policy that would be scouted by ourselves. But we must be ruled by circumstances. If crimes are un-English—if English means for detecting and punishing them fail, why should not an un-English power be exercised in districts where violence and murder stalk unavenged and unchecked?[69]

"The great obstacle to tranquillity in Ireland," exclaimed the self-righteous *Times,* "is the national character—the character of the masses, of the middle classes, of the senators of Ireland. . . . Their very virtues in their extravagance become vices too." Accordingly, the newspaper reasoned, the Irish were as yet unfit for the blessings of the British Constitution. Ireland was getting only what she deserved—poverty, distress, coercive legislation and repressive administration. "When Ireland acts according to the principles of civilised man, then she can be ruled by the laws of civilised man."[70]

Notes

1. John Stuart Mill, *Principles of Political Economy with Some of Their Applications to Social Philosophy* (Boston, 1848), Vol. I, 369.

2. *The Times*, August 4, 1843, and January 26, 1847.

3. *Ibid.*, October 25, 1845.

4. *Fraser's Magazine*, XXXVI (March 1847), 373.

5. *Punch*, XIV (1849), 54; XVII (1851), 26, 231.

6. Phillip Luckombe, *A Tour Through Ireland: Wherein the Present State of That Kingdom Is Considered; and the Most Noted Cities, Towns, Seats, Buildings, Loughs, Etc. Described . . .* (London, 1783), 19.

7. Dr. Duncan of Liverpool, quoted in an anonymous pamphlet, *Observations on the Habits of the Labouring Classes in Ireland. Suggested by Mr. C. C. Lewis' Report on the State of the Irish Poor in Great Britain* (Dublin, 1836), 9. The author of this pamphlet challenges the Irish assertion that Irishmen, like Englishmen, would have a higher standard of living if they were better paid. Irishmen, he suggests, would waste any additional income on drink and it is therefore preferable to pay them lower salaries.

8. James Page, *Ireland: Its Evils Traced to Their Source* (London, 1836), Vol. I, 10.

9. Henrietta G. Chatterton, *Rambles in the South of Ireland* (London, 1839), Vol. I, 10.

10. *Fraser's Magazine*, XXXVI (March 1847), 373.

11. *The Times*, December 8, 1843.

12. *Blackwood's Magazine*, LIX (May 1846), 600, 602.

13. For further documentation of this argument, see Richard Ned Lebow, "British Images of Poverty in Pre-Famine Ireland," in Daniel Casey and Richard Rhodes, eds., *The Irish Peasant in the Nineteenth Century* (forthcoming).

14. *Hansard's Parliamentary Debates*, third series, LXIX (1843), cols. 1010–1011 (hereafter referred to as *Hansard's*).

15. George Poulett Thomason Scrope, *How Is Ireland to Be Governed?* (London, 1834), 20–21.

16. John Carr, *The Stranger in Ireland: or, A Tour in the Southern and Western Parts of That Country in the Year 1805* (Philadelphia, 1806), 151.

17. *Punch*, I (1841), 153; XIV (1849), 214; II (1842), 83.

18. John Barrow, *A Tour Round Ireland* (London, 1836), 35.

19. James Johnson, *A Tour in Ireland; With Meditations and Reflections* (London, 1844), 144.

20. Thomas Crofton Croker, *Researches in the South of Ireland* (London, 1824), Vol. I, 33–34.

21. Thomas Walford, *The Scientific Tourist Through Ireland . . . by an Irish Gentleman* (London, 1818), 44.

22. *The Times*, December 2, 1845.

23. *Ibid.*, October 13, 1846.

24. Robert Peel to James Graham, December 3, 1845, in the Peel Papers (British Museum), Add. Mss. 40452.

25. *Hansard's*, LXIX (1843), cols. 1175–1186.

26. *Ibid.*, col. 1001.

27. Quoted in J. C. Colquhoun, *Ireland; Popery and Priestcraft the Cause of Her Misery and Crime* (Glasgow, 1836), 4.

28. Thomas Babington Macaulay, *The History of England from the Accession of James II* (London, 1884), Vol. III, 146–147. See also his speeches before Parliament, especially *Repeal of the Union with Ireland: A Speech . . . Delivered in the House of Commons . . .* (Dublin, 1886).

29. Nassau William Senior, *Journals, Conversations and Essays Relating to Ireland* (London, 1868), Vol. I, 70–72.

30. Page, *Ireland: Its Evils Traced to Their Source*, 6.

31. *The Times*, November 12, 1844.

32. *Punch*, V (1843), 134; II (1842), 50, 136.

33. Stanley Morison, ed., *History of The Times* (London, 1939), Vol. II, 8; Robert Blake, *Disraeli* (London, 1966), 132.

34. *The Times*, June 16, 1836.

35. Angus Macintyre, *The Liberator: Daniel O'Connell and the Irish Party, 1830–1847* (New York, 1965), 155–157.

36. Quoted in *ibid.*, 47.

37. Duke of Wellington to Robert Peel, February 20, 1837, in the Peel Papers, Add. Mss. 40423.

38. Kevin Nowlan, *The Politics of Repeal: A Study in the Relations Between Great Britain and Ireland, 1841–1850* (London, 1965), 14.

39. Charles Greville, *Greville Memoirs, Part II: A Journal of the Reign of Queen Victoria from 1837–1852* (London, 1885), Vol. I, 2, 27, 279–280.

40. Sir Herbert Eustace Maxwell, ed., *Life and Letters of George William*

Frederick Villiers, the Fourth Earl of Clarendon (London, 1913), Vol. I, 278.

41. Marquess of Anglesey to Lord Melbourne, December 31, 1840, from the Plas Newydd Papers, quoted in Macintyre, *The Liberator,* 21.

42. *Punch,* IX (1845), 45, 215, 218.

43. *The Times,* January 24, 1843.

44. *Ibid.,* June 5, 1843.

45. *Ibid.*

46. Edward Plunkett, *Address to the Landowners of Ireland upon the Present Agitation for a Repeal of the Union* (London, 1843), 17–18.

47. *Hansard's,* LXXI (1843), col. 430.

48. *The Times,* June 1, 1843.

49. *Thoughts on Ireland* (London, 1847), 6.

50. Page, *Ireland: Its Evils Traced to Their Source,* 17.

51. *Hansard's,* LXXXIV (1846), cols. 1413–1414.

52. *Ibid.,* col. 1414.

53. Henry Cooke, *Authentic Report of the Speech of . . . at the Great Protestant Meeting, Hillsborough* (Belfast, 1834), 9.

54. Nowlan, *The Politics of Repeal,* 65–66, 110, 177–178.

55. *Hansard's,* LIII (1840), cols. 87–88.

56. *Ibid.,* LXII (1843), col. 698.

57. *Ibid.,* col. 367.

58. *The Times,* April 18, 1836 (Letter XVI of the Runnymede Letters); Robert Blake, *Disraeli* (London, 1966), 132.

59. Quoted in Macintyre, *The Liberator,* 239 n.

60. *Blackwood's Magazine,* LIX (May 1846), 573.

61. *Ibid.,* LI (April 1842), 509; LXII (July–December 1847), 725.

62. *Ibid.,* LXIII (January–June 1848), 122.

63. Richard M. Hassard, *Popery, as It Is, and Will Be, Until Destroyed . . .* (Dublin, 1839), frontispiece.

64. Colquhoun, *Ireland,* 19.

65. *Freeman's Journal,* January 30, 1843.

66. *Blackwood's Magazine,* LIX (May 1846), 527.

67. *The Times,* June 13, 1843, and September 1, 1843.

68. *Fraser's Magazine,* XXXIV (October 1845), 499.

69. *The Times,* December 2, 1846.

70. *Ibid.,* March 30, 1846.

CHAPTER 5

A Perceptual Prison

> *What harm to Ireland does England intend or knowingly inflict? What good, that she knows how to give her, would she not willingly bestow? Unhappily, her offence is precisely that she does not know, and is so well contented with not knowing, that Irishmen who are not hostile to her are coming to believe that she will not and cannot learn.*
>
> JOHN STUART MILL

The British political elite and electorate failed to develop sympathy for the plight of the Irish people. Even the majority of the organs of public opinion in the forefront of reform at home remained deaf to the pleas of the Repeal movement; and some went so far as to take up the cudgels of reaction and to support the very measures in Ireland that they opposed in Britain. Thus public opinion in Britain failed to provide a countervailing force to Ireland's Anglo-Protestant minority, which, unchecked, further depressed the condition of Ireland.

Why did public opinion espouse the need for reform in Britain and abroad but not in Ireland? Why did oppressive and exploitative policies in Ireland—which eventually undermined

British rule in that country—continue to receive the sanction of successive British governments without any widespread opposition from the British electorate?

One possible explanation is the strategic importance of Ireland to Britain at that time. Ireland had always proved to be the weakest link in the chain of British defenses against invasion. Spaniards and, later, Frenchmen had attempted to instigate revolution in Ireland and had supported uprisings with money and arms. Ireland was a tinder box which, when touched by any spark thrown off by a European conflagration, burst into flame, threatening to destroy British power. No British administration, Whig or Tory, could allow Ireland to become independent of British control.

In the years prior to the great famine this problem was considered important by successive British governments because France was still regarded as a power with possible ambitions of dominance. In the 1840s tensions between the two nations were not particularly acute but the possibility of war was not altogether to be discounted. For this reason the strategic importance of Ireland and Britain's need to maintain her power over that island were more significant to the political elite than any contradiction between the emerging value consensus in British society and the means through which British power in Ireland was maintained.

Yet the maintenance of British power and responsiveness to the needs of the Irish people were by no means mutually exclusive. O'Connell and his Radical allies suggested not only that the two goals were compatible but that the latter was necessary in order to guarantee the former. They argued that British security could best be guaranteed by winning the support of the Irish people for the Union with Britain. Pointing to the government's willingness to adopt such a policy of reconciliation toward Canada, they argued its application to Ireland as well.

O'Connell never declared repeal of the Union to be a nonnegotiable demand until the policies of successive governments forced him to conclude that the Irish people would never gain satisfaction from the British parliament. Prior to this point of no return—reached only with the onset of the famine—O'Connell considered Repeal to be but one of several means through which justice and good government in Ireland could be achieved. Unlike later Irish nationalists, he was perfectly willing to abandon agitation for Repeal—as he did during his alliance with the Whigs—if meaningful reform could be achieved within the format of the Act of Union.

Repeal was not necessarily a threat to British security. While O'Connell was guilty of never defining the institutional arrangements that would govern the relations between the two countries after Repeal, he clearly never demanded total independence. Rather, Repealers insisted on the creation of an Irish parliament with authority over the *domestic* affairs of the country, a constitutional arrangement not dissimilar to the one that had prevailed prior to the Act of Union.

Thus democratization of Irish politics would not necessarily have prejudiced British strategic interests; even the grant of Repeal could have been harmonized with considerations of security. What is significant is not the *logical* compatibility of British interests and Irish demands, but rather their *perceptual* incompatibility in the minds of contemporary Englishmen.

The Growth of an Image

The results of this study suggest that neither Repeal nor any of the policies likely to promote reconciliation between Britain and the mass of the Irish people was seen as a reasonable alternative by either political party or by the majority of the British electorate. The British perception of Irish affairs was dominated by an image of Irishmen that resisted change despite contradictory evidence and that limited the policy alternatives considered acceptable with regard to Ireland. The image tended to function as a perceptual prison, blinding many decision makers and much of the electorate to the wide range of feasible alternatives. It led Englishmen to conclude that most of the grievances voiced by the Irish were imaginary, that the political organizers were insincere about their motives and dishonest about their goals and that "law and order," not concession, was the proper policy to pursue toward Ireland. The historical development of this stereotype spanned the centuries of British rule in Ireland. Its eventual transformation into a perceptual prison can be characterized in three stages: conscious innovation, self-fulfillment and self-justification.

CONSCIOUS INNOVATION

The stereotypic characterization of Irishmen actually dated back to the twelfth century, when Irish "barbarism" and "paganism" provided the pretext for the invasion of that country by Henry II. Twelfth-century Ireland was in a state of political turmoil with various factions fighting unsuccessfully to unite the country. The constant warfare weakened Ireland in relation to her predatory neighbors and tempted the Normans to invade in 1169. Henry of England, jealous not only of Irish independence but of Norman power, sought to press his own claims over the country. He turned to the papacy for support.

The Irish occupied a unique place in Western Christendom; alone among the churches of Western Europe the Irish organization was independent of Rome. To provide a pretext for the invasion Henry sent defamatory reports of Irish customs and religious practices to Rome and offered to subdue Ireland in order to bring both civilization and Christianity to its people. The ploy was successful since the Holy See was anxious to secure Irish fealty. Hadrian IV, the one English pope, issued the Bull Laudabiliter sanctioning the invasion. In this document Hadrian portrayed Henry as "a Catholic Prince labouring to extend the borders of the Church and teach the truth of the Christian faith to a rude and unlettered people." In return the king swore "to enter Ireland in order to subdue the people and make them obedient to the laws, and that he is willing to pay from every house there one penny to St. Peter and to keep and preserve the rights of the churches in that land whole and inviolate."[1]

Henry's claim that Ireland's people were heathen and uncivilized was, no doubt, so contradictory to contemporary impressions, still influenced by memories of past Irish glories, that he felt the need to supply supporting evidence. With this end in mind he dispatched a Welsh monk, Giraldus Cambrensis, to Ireland with instructions to "gather evidence" in support of his claim. Cambrensis, whose *History of the Conquest of Ireland* became the major source on early Ireland for five centuries of British historians, served his master well. He described the "wild Irish" as eaters of human flesh, murderers and thieves who reveled in sodomy and incest. Irish religion, in his opinion, was a superstitious doctrine that bore no relationship to Christianity. It consisted of pagan beliefs couched in a nominally Christian form that served only to guarantee the ascendancy of the bards and uncivilized priests over the ignorant people. Rather than soothing the soul, the religion incited the people to the most wanton cruelty and was primarily responsible for their degraded character. Cambrensis found the natives totally lacking in moral development of any kind:

> No realme, no nation, no state, nor commonwealth throughout all Europe, can yeeld more nor so manie profitable lawes, direction, rules, examples and discourses . . . than doe the histories of this little Isle of Britanne or England. I would to God I might or were able to saithe like or halfe like of Ireland, a countrie, the more barren of good things, the more replenished with actions of bloud, murther, and louthsome outrages; which to anie good reader are greevous and irksome to be read and considered.[2]

SELF-FULFILLMENT

The conquest of Ireland led to its eventual colonization by growing numbers of settlers, administrators and soldiers. Intent on realizing quick profits, they gradually expropriated the land from the native inhabitants and reduced them to a state of political and economic dependence. The Reformation, which aggravated the already existing hostility between the native Irish and their alien conquerors, provided a further rationale for depriving the Irish of wealth and influence.* The

*The religious wars of the sixteenth and seventeenth centuries have left the impression that the Reformation and the ensuing religious differences between the English and the Irish were at the root of the "Irish problem." However, the crucial distinction was not between Protestant and Catholic but between "Saxon" and "Celt." Evidence for this assertion can be drawn from the fact that Englishmen rarely explained the failings of the Irish character in terms of the effects of Catholicism but, vice versa, explained the Irish refusal to embrace Protestantism in terms of the degraded character of the Celt. John Temple, an eighteenth-century Englishman whose writings on Ireland were widely quoted by later generations, took care to stress this point. Temple declared that

> the malignant impressions of Irreligion and barbarism, transmitted down, whether by infusion from the ancestors, or natural generation, had irrefagably [sic] stiffened their necks, and hardened their hearts against all the most powerful endeavours of *Reformation:* they continued one and the same in all their wicked customs and inclinations, without change in their affections or manners, having their eyes inflamed, their hearts enraged with malice and hatred against all the English nation, breathing forth nothing but their ruin, destruction, and utter extirpation [*The Irish Rebellion . . .* (London, 1746), 19].

The historian and philosopher David Hume also subscribed to this view. In his *History of England* Hume explained why the Irish remained Catholic in face of the Reformation that transformed Britain and most of northern Europe:

> As the rudeness and ignorance of the Irish were extreme, they were sunk below the reach of that curiousity and love of novelty by which every other people in Europe had been seized at the beginning of that century and which had engaged them in innovations and religious disputes, with which they were still violently agitated. The ancient superstitions, the practices and observances of their fathers, mingled and polluted with many wild

stereotype of the Irish, by now widely accepted in both Britain and Ireland, proved functional in reducing whatever dissonance developed by reason of the contradiction between Christian values and the manner in which the Irish were treated. It also legitimated continued British rule in Ireland.

Psychologists have suggested that the expectation of certain behavior evokes that very behavior in countless subtle ways. If a child is said to be stupid and is continually treated as such, it is unlikely, regardless of his native ability, that he will do well in school. If a man believes that his colleagues are hostile toward him he is likely to act in such a defensive manner as to provoke true hostility. The same mechanism operates with respect to group prejudice. Initial prejudice triggers a certain sort of behavior toward the out-group, behavior based on the prevailing stereotype. This may make it practical for the out-group to exhibit or develop some of the characteristics attributed to it by the stereotype. Therefore stereotypes frequently involve a "self-fulfilling prophecy." Gordon Allport, reviewing the literature on prejudice, suggests: "Too often we think of out-groups as simply possessing certain qualities and in-groups as having certain false images of these qualities. The truth of the matter is that these two conditions interact."[3]

Over the centuries the stereotype of the Irish, like other social stereotypes, became at least in part self-fulfilling. To begin with, British perceptions of the Irish influenced British policy toward Ireland in many ways. One telling example concerns the British response to the great potato famine of 1845–1852. Given its image of the lazy Irish, the Russell administra-

---

opinions, still maintained an unshaken empire over them; and the example alone of the English was sufficient to render the reformation odious to the prejudices of the discontented Irish. The old opposition of manners, laws, and interests was now inflamed by religious antipathy; and the subduing and civilizing of that country seemed to become every day more difficult and impracticable [*History of England* (London, 1778), Vol. V, 397–398].

tion was reluctant to make outdoor relief too appealing, lest millions of Irish, receiving the basic requisites for survival, find no incentive to seek employment. Relief had to be made unattractive. One method of doing this was the introduction of a means test whereby any Irishman owning more than one-quarter acre of land was forced to give up title to his holding before being placed on the relief rolls. In practice this robbed the peasant of his most likely means of escaping from the charity of the government—a successful harvest on his plot of land. The assumption that the Irish would exploit British charity fostered a policy that left them little other choice.

By the nineteenth century the major characteristics attributed to the Irish—indolence, superstition, dishonesty and a propensity to violence—had remained prominent in the British image for over six hundred years. There can be no doubt that by then the Irish displayed many of these characteristics to a greater extent than did their English neighbors. The centuries of oppression and discrimination made it functional—both psychologically and economically—for them to behave in such a manner. One perceptive English traveler who toured Ireland in the latter half of the eighteenth century commented:

> We keep the Irish dark and ignorant, and then we wonder how they can be so enthralled by superstition; we make them poor and unhappy, and then we wonder that they are so prone to tumult and disorder; we tie up their hands, so that they have no inducements to industry, and then we wonder they are so lazy and indolent. No wonder that it should be part of the Irish character that they are so *careless of their lives*, when they have so little worth living for.[4]

If the Irish were indolent, the British had most assuredly encouraged them to be so. All too often, an Irishman who improved his land was either charged more rent or expelled to make room for another tenant who would pay a higher rent. John Stuart Mill, a lifelong crusader against the Irish land system, declared:

Almost alone amongst mankind the cottier is in the condition that he can scarcely be any better or worse off by any act of his own. If he were industrious or prudent, nobody but his landlord would gain; if he is lazy or intemperate, it is at his landlord's expense.[5]

If the Irish were superstitious, once again British policy had helped to guarantee that they would be so. Under the Penal Laws the government forbade Irish Catholics from being educated outside of Ireland, outlawed Catholic education within Ireland and persecuted the church and its adherents. Over time, the intellectual level of the clergy declined, but the power of the religion over the people increased. The church was their one remaining native institution; its very existence was an act of defiance to the alien conqueror. The very power it came to wield derived largely from the persecution it suffered at the hands of the British. Richard Cobden suggested that this persecution did for the church what nothing else could have.[6]

Perhaps the most important self-validating aspect of the stereotype was the proverbial Irish hatred of Britain and the willingness of the population to rebel when given the opportunity. Since they were often treated like treacherous rebels, it should not be surprising that the Irish became more defiant over the years. British observers who traced the appeal of the Repeal movement to this Irish characteristic explained it in terms of the perverse nature of the Celt. In reality, the British conquest had made the histories of the two countries so much the reverse of each other that they came to resemble a zero-sum game. What to an Englishman meant glory, victory and prosperity, to an Irishman spelled misery, degradation and ruin. One present-day commentator has written:

In Ireland the name of Elizabeth I stands only for the horrors of the Irish conquest; in the defeat of the Armada, Ireland's hope of independence went down; above all, with the name of William III and the glorious revolution of 1688, the very foundation of

HEIGHT OF IMPUDENCE.

In the original caption the Irishman says to John Bull: "Spare a thrifle, yer Honour, for a poor Irish Lad to buy a bit of—a Blunderbuss with." From *Punch* (1846).

British liberties, the Catholic Irishman associates only the final subjection of his country and the degradation and injustice of the penal laws. Freedom for the one meant defeat for the other; the good of the one was the evil of the other. Ireland, resentful and hostile, lying only a day's sail in fine weather, from Britain's coasts, for centuries provided a refuge for enemy agents, a hatching-ground for enemy plots; her motto was "England's difficulty is Ireland's opportunity," and in every crisis of England's history she seized the moment of weakness to stab her enemy in the back.[7]

To the Irish a rebellion was a blow struck for freedom. To the British it was treachery, confirming their image of the barbaric, violent and, worst of all, ungrateful Celt, who abused the advantages offered to him by Britain. In the aftermath of such a struggle the British reaction was usually severe and made future rebellion even more likely.

SELF-JUSTIFICATION

What had begun as a largely imaginary thing in the minds of Henry II and his supporters became ever more a social reality. Over the centuries the image came to dominate the perception of Englishmen who had never even visited Ireland. The image had spread from Ireland to England with the steady stream of commentaries, travel descriptions and reports written by colonists, administrators and casual visitors to Ireland. Englishmen were conditioned to expect the Irish to behave in a specified manner. When they came to Ireland they brought their preconceived notions of the Irish with them, and since the image had become in part an actuality, they had little difficulty in finding a confirmation of their beliefs. Their subsequent writings and conversations reinforced the stereotype and helped to tighten its grip on the British mind. In this way the stereotype produced its own support or justification. By the nineteenth century, the evidence suggests, it had become a perceptual prison, a closed image by which information about

Ireland was organized and given meaning and in terms of which policy was frequently formulated.

With the final stage, self-justification, the circle was completed:

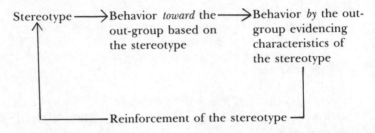

In his pioneering study of race relations in the United States Gunnar Myrdal illustrates how this pernicious circle may work:

> White prejudice and discrimination keep the Negro low in standards of living, health, education, manners and morals. This, in its turn, gives support to white prejudice. White prejudice and Negro standards thus mutually "cause" each other. . . .
>
> The low plane of living, the cultural isolation, and all the resulting bodily, intellectual, and moral disabilities and distortions of the average Negro make it natural for the ordinary white man not only to see that the Negro is inferior but also to believe honestly that the Negro's inferiority is inborn. This belief means, of course, that all attempts to improve the Negro by education, health reforms, or merely by giving him his rights as a worker and a citizen must seem to be less promising of success than they otherwise would be. The Negro is judged to be fundamentally incorrigible, and he is, therefore, kept in a slum existence which, in its turn, leaves the imprint upon his body and soul which makes it natural for the white man to believe in his inferiority.[8]

When British policy is examined in light of the Irish stereotype it becomes apparent that it was not entirely hypocritical. While self-interest and political expediency were often quite conscious elements of policy formulation, it is probably fair to say that most decision makers in Victorian England did not perceive the steady contradiction between their policies and the avowed goal of reconciliation with Ireland.

The British people honestly condemned oppression in other parts of the world but remained blind to its existence in their own back yard. The sufferings of Algerian *fellahin*, Polish peasants and Russian Jews evoked the sympathy of the British people, but they remained relatively unmoved by the cries of the Irish. The revolutions of Greeks, Poles, Hungarians and Italians drew their support and fired their imagination; the rebellion of Irishmen brought forth only their incomprehension and ire. John Stuart Mill, writing of the British reaction to the Fenian rebellion of the 1860s, remarked ruefully:

> Alas for the self-complacent ignorance of irresponsible rulers, be they monarchs, classes, or nations! If there is anything sadder than the calamity itself, it is the unmistakable sincerity and good faith with which numbers of Englishmen confess themselves incapable of comprehending it. They know not that the dissaffection, which neither has nor needs any other motive than aversion to the rulers, is the climax of a long growth of dissaffection arising from causes that might have been removed. What seems to them the causelessness of the Irish repugnance to our rule, is the proof that they have almost let pass the last opportunity they are ever likely to have of setting it right.[9]

The Pace of Demand and Concession

Between 1800 and 1916 the success of the Union depended upon the outcome of the race between Irish demands and British concessions. The crucial question is not whether Irish demands were met—because eventually they all were—but rather at what point each reform was made. The major Irish grievances were rectified by Catholic emancipation in 1829, the Irish Franchise Acts of 1850 and 1884, disestablishment of the Church of Ireland in 1869, the Land Reform Act of 1870 and, finally, the Home Rule Bill of 1913. Nevertheless, each act, coming along after the reform had been demanded, was too late to produce Irish reconciliation to British rule.

Catholic emancipation was granted in 1829—after a twenty-year struggle which robbed it of any significance it might have had as a conciliatory gesture. Since it was extracted from Parliament by the threat of revolution, the Irish perceived it to be a victory won by blood rather than a measure of conciliation toward the Irish people. Moreover, it was stripped of much of its value by the corresponding disenfranchisement of most of the Catholic electorate of Ireland. This grievance was corrected only in 1884 with the extension of manhood suffrage to most of Ireland.

Disestablishment met with a similar reception. The Church of Ireland was deprived of its special privileges only after the bloody uprising of the Fenians. Disestablishment was enacted to prevent revolution; it was not a concession motivated by a desire to do justice to Ireland. If disestablishment had been enacted thirty years before it might have had considerable effect on the mass of the Irish people. By 1869 it appeared to be merely a long-overdue rectification of an ancient injustice.

Land reform was similarly late in coming. If it had been introduced in the thirties or forties and the Irish peasants transformed into peasant proprietors, a major grievance would have been redressed. Repeal and agrarian outrages would have lost their impetus and the Irish people might have become reconciled to the Union. No doubt, much of the suffering caused by the great potato famine could have been averted if this reform had been enacted in time, and the revolution of 1848 would probably have been stillborn. However, land reform was enacted not in 1840 but in 1870, and like emancipation it took back with one hand what it gave with the other. By that time the transformation of British agriculture had threatened the economic viability of Irish estates, and the profits of Irish landowners were precipitously declining. The Land Reform Act enabled these proprietors to leave Ireland at a particularly auspicious time. It guaranteed that their land would be sold at a price above what it would have fetched on the open market. Accordingly, the act hardly impressed the Irish people with Britain's concern for their well-being.

Home rule conformed to the same pattern. If it had been granted in 1840 or even in 1860 revolution would most likely not have occurred in Ireland. It finally received the royal assent in 1913, only to be shelved because of the world war. Once again Irishmen did not perceive the government's action as a concession motivated by a sincere desire to appease the Irish people, but rather as a delayed recognition of their status, achieved only by blood and suffering. The fact that the reform was postponed angered them even more and led to the futile Easter Rebellion of 1916.

In each case Great Britain eventually gave the Irish people what they asked for, but refused to concede the point until it was too late for any conciliatory effect. By the time the British government had awarded emancipation, disestablishment, land reform, home rule or, indeed, any other measure, its only effect was to rekindle the flames of resentment and alienation.

The pernicious operation of the British stereotype of the Irish was responsible in part for the time lag between Irish demands and British concessions. The stereotype so blinded the British people to the validity of Irish demands and the justice of the Irish cause that they were unable to perceive the necessity of taking action until it was too late. Before British opinion came to support Irish reform it was necessary to strip away the veil clouding the perception of Irish affairs. This gradual process failed to keep pace with the needs of policy.

In time, the discrepancy between the stereotype and the reality grew more apparent as the contradictions between the values of British society and the means used to govern Ireland increased. Continual agitation by a vocal and growing British minority intent on rectifying past injustices to Ireland eventually had an effect. Little by little, the hold of the stereotype was weakened, and the British people came to perceive Irish affairs in a more realistic manner. However, the process took time and the lag between demands and concessions was so great that the British attempt to maintain the connection with Ireland inevitably had to fail. On a directly political level it might be said that the stereotype functioned to increase the power of the Orange party—that faction most opposed to change and reform in Ireland—far beyond its intrinsic political strength. The hold of the stereotype over the British public enabled Orange spokesmen to mobilize popular support for their position. At the same time, it decreased the power of Repealers—and later, Irish nationalists—by making their demands unacceptable to a majority of the British electorate.

Evidence for this can be seen in the failure of O'Connell's compact with the Whigs in the 1830s. The Irish-Catholic faction was important to the Whig majority in Parliament, but the Whigs were unable to meet Irish demands without antagonizing the majority of their non-Irish supporters. As a result, O'Connell and the Repeal party gained little from the alliance. A more graphic illustration of this political fact was Gladstone's attempt to form an alliance with Parnell. The British electorate was so opposed to the proposed grant of home rule that the alliance destroyed the unity of the Liberal Party. The right wing of the party defected to the Tories—now known as the Unionists—and brought the incumbent government down from power. The goals of the Irish party remained outside the British political spectrum, and as a result its parliamentary influence was not as great as that of other, numerically weaker factions whose goals were well within the accepted spectrum.

Thus the stereotyped image of Irishmen, a concomitant of colonial rule in Ireland, also proved to be a major factor in the undoing of colonial rule. The stereotype reduced dissonance but did so at the expense of an accurate perception of political and social reality in Ireland. It rendered Britain unable to pursue that course most likely to preserve her influence in Ireland.

Notes

1. Quoted in Edmund Curtis, *A History of Ireland,* 5th ed. (London, 1950), 57.

2. Giraldus Cambrensis, *The Irish Historie Composed and Written by Giraldus Cambrensis, and Translated into English* . . . , *by John Hooker* . . . , Vol. II of Raphael Holinshed et al., *The First and Second Volumes of Chronicles* . . . (London, 1577), Epistle Dedicatore.

3. Gordon W. Allport, *The Nature of Prejudice* (Garden City, N.Y., 1958), 156. See also Robert K. Merton, "The Self-Fulfilling Prophecy," *Antioch Review,* VIII (1948), 193–210.

4. Thomas Campbell, *A Philosophical Survey of the South of Ireland* . . . (Dublin, 1778), 253.

5. John Stuart Mill, *Principles of Political Economy with Some of Their Applications to Social Philosophy* (Boston, 1848), Vol. II, 283.

6. Richard Cobden, *England, Ireland and America* (London, 1836).

7. Cecil Woodham-Smith, *The Great Hunger* (New York, 1962), 19.

8. Gunnar Myrdal et al., *An American Dilemma: The Negro Problem and Modern Democracy* (New York, 1944), pp. 75, 101.

9. John Stuart Mill, *England and Ireland* (London, 1868), 6–7.

CHAPTER 6

Colonial Policies and Their Payoffs

Goals and Strategies of a Colonial Power

The central concern of any metropolitan power seeking to maintain control of a colony must be to minimize the opposition of the indigenous population. The strategies adopted to achieve this end are a function of the goals toward which colonial rule is directed.

In the nineteenth century all colonial powers, like Britain in Ireland, were presented with two alternative sets of goals. The traditional conception of empire envisaged colonies as territories to be exploited. A newer conception, not fully articulated until after the French Revolution, was that colonies provided additional land and people whose integration into the political unit would strengthen the nation. The former conception relied upon superior military power to keep the people quiescent; the latter, upon responsiveness to make them loyal.

Unlike many political questions of the nineteenth century, this one did not lend itself to a compromise that would partially fulfill both conceptions. The alternative goals were by their very nature mutually exclusive. If colonial powers desired to maintain their empires they were compelled to make a choice between the two. An examination of the strategies required to implement the goals will help to illustrate the increasing dilemma faced by metropolitan powers.

A strategy of coercion is dictated by a goal of exploitation. To the extent that the colony is exploited at the expense of the inhabitants the colonizer must rely upon his superior power to preserve control. Such a strategy requires a minimal material commitment, can lead to an immediate "payoff," but is less likely to result in a stable political connection.

The colonizer's authority depends on his ability to enforce obedience by the subject population. The colonized must be made to realize that rebellion is doomed to failure or entails intolerable cost to the insurgents. The payoff of such a strategy is both material and psychological. The metropolitan power can exact tribute or forced labor, exploit the material wealth and economic resources of the colony and utilize its geographic position for military advantage vis-à-vis other powers. A coercion strategy is also rewarding in the sense that domination gained through force and control exercised through terror enable individuals, classes or societies to give expression to inner frustrations and anxieties.[1]

The drawbacks of basing authority on coercion are manifold. The colonizer's authority is likely to be accepted only as long as his power and his will to use it remain unquestioned. Should the metropolitan country suffer a relative decline in power by reason of internal disruption or foreign conflict, or should the colonized territory redress the military imbalance by securing the support of a third power, the danger of rebellion will increase. The Irish, for example, remained poised for rebellion throughout the centuries before the Union. Actual insurgency occurred, however, only when military factors favored the chances of rebellion. In 1640, when Britain was internally divided by civil war, in 1690, when it was threatened by Louis XIV, and again in 1798, when it was locked in a deadly struggle with Napoleon, the Irish capitalized upon Britain's weakness and the opportunity for foreign support and rose in rebellion.

The colonizer's authority is equally likely to be challenged should he grow "soft," his military spirit dampened by the spoils of success, by the rigor of frequent battle or by changes in the ethics of his society. This was, no doubt, an important calculation of the leaders of the Irish insurrection in 1920–1921.

Colonies ruled by such methods can present the specter of constant rebellion. If the power of the colonizer is called into question for any of the reasons discussed, the cost of preserving domination may become so high as to offset the profit extracted from the colony. In the case of Ireland this probably occurred some time in the middle of the nineteenth century. While maintenance can develop into a costly burden, withdrawal may be perceived as an even more disastrous outcome because of the precedent it could set for other, similar situations—the domino theory—or because it would leave behind a hostile population likely to pose a threat to the former colonizer. Both of these considerations were paramount in the minds of those Englishmen who opposed repeal of the Union.

The rather Machiavellian moral to be learned from this dilemma is that rule based on coercion must never be allowed to be questioned to the extent that a serious threat to domination develops. There are two means which can be employed to prevent such a situation from arising.

The most commonly adopted course is aimed at preserving the colonizer's credibility by terror and violence. This has been the standard technique resorted to by most conquerors. Genghis Khan, for example, was so effective in terrorizing the Russian princes and people during his brief campaigns in Russia that when the hordes retired behind the Asian steppes they considered it unnecessary to leave behind a force of occupation. In the hundred years that followed Russian strength vis-à-vis the Tartars steadily increased but the yearly tribute to Astrakhan was nevertheless dutifully delivered for fear of the consequences should it be withheld.

In the modern world the use of terror and violence as a deterrent has lost much of its efficacy. The maintenance of the colonizer's credibility in the eyes of the native population is in itself no longer effective in preventing rebellion. When struggles take on ideological significance the level of endurance of all the participants is raised. Action is inspired that is frequently suicidal in cost. When people rebel in the name of religious freedom, human liberty or national independence, the extent of their opponent's destructive capacity is no longer the most relevant consideration because the insurgents no longer perceive death as the worst of all possible outcomes. The Russian boyars would have dismissed as absurd the suggestion that they begin a futile rebellion for the sake of national honor. But the Irishmen who calmly faced death in the springtime of their lives in the Easter Rebellion of 1916 did so willingly. The insurgency began with a conscious recognition on their part that it was doomed to failure. The cry of "Give me liberty or give me death"—or the more contemporary "Better dead than red"—reflects the transcendent importance ideological principles occupy in the modern individual's value hierarchy.

If the politically relevant population of the colony can no longer be effectively controlled by the destructive capability of the colonizer, the only recourse likely to be effective in preserving domination is a policy designed to prevent the development of an elite capable of leading a revolution. Perhaps the ultimate application of this logic is to be found in Hitler's projected plans for eastern Europe.

The Nazis intended to exterminate a large percentage of the native population, including all those who had received an education. German settlers were to repopulate the land, while the remaining inhabitants were to be reduced to hewers of wood and drawers of water, mere slaves who would carry out necessary but menial agricultural and mechanical labor. Deprived of organizational and military skills, illiterate and uneducated, the population would have been transformed into beasts of burden, human only in their physical form and potential. Such a population—assuming it had no contact with the outside world—would have posed little threat to the German ascendancy.

At the opposite end of the political spectrum from the strategy of coercion is the strategy designed to integrate the colonial population into the national political community. The aim of this strategy is to secure the loyalty of the colonial subjects by legitimizing the colonial connection in their eyes.

A political system develops legitimacy when it is consistently able to meet the needs and fulfill the expectations of the population over which it wields authority. The more often its ability in this regard is demonstrated over time, the more the people come to associate their individual success with the success and survival of the system. As support for the system grows, its authority to make decisions affecting the lives and fortunes of the population is less frequently questioned. Compliance gradually becomes a habit.

A political system derives great advantages from having secured the loyalty of the population. Among other things, it obtains a certain degree of latitude for its actions by reason of the reservoir of support it has built up. This support, a credit that can be drawn upon during times of crisis, enables the system to survive reverses which otherwise might have proved fatal.

Legitimacy, however, is more difficult to achieve than rule based on coercion, and it entails a higher expenditure of resources. A heavy load is placed on the decision-making apparatus of the metropolitan power. Its institutions must develop means to judge the needs of the population and must be capable of bringing the resources of the state to bear where they are required. This in itself requires a considerable expenditure of time, money and effort. In addition, these resources must be expended over a long period of time before any payoff becomes apparent. Scholars who have studied the integration process have found that the advantages the colonized community derives from amalgamation must outweigh the burdens. It is only after the colony's politically relevant population perceives that it is likely to attain a higher degree of wealth, status, honor and security by virtue of integration, and in fact realizes these goals, that it is likely to assume the responsibilities of the relationship.[2]

Perhaps the most difficult commitment is of a psychological nature. The colonizer cannot preserve his exclusiveness and sense of superiority over the colonized if meaningful social contact and communication are to be established. Without such communication it is impossible to develop the mutual understanding, trust and predictability of behavior that are so essential to responsiveness. No level of administrative capability and material expenditure will compensate for the lack. Unless a high degree of empathy develops, the metropolitan society will most likely be extremely reluctant to consent to the high cost of a strategy of integration and to grant the opportunities for upward mobility so essential to that strategy's success.

Herein lies the danger of the strategy of integration. If for any reason the metropolitan power proves unresponsive to the needs of the colonized or fails to create the mobility that the population has been led to expect, the integration will be unsuccessful. The colonial power will have created expectations that have not been fulfilled and probably will alienate the community it sought to integrate. In such a case, as in Ireland, rebellion or at least agitation for autonomy is likely to develop.

Ironically, the probability for the success of a rebellion is likely to be considerably greater than if the metropolitan power had never attempted integration. Unlike a coercive strategy, which aims to prevent a native elite from developing, a strategy designed to achieve integration encourages mobility and political participation. An unsuccessful attempt at integration, by providing some mobility and some political participation, will create an elite without at the same time securing the loyalties of that elite to the larger political unit. The very cadres necessary to organize and carry out rebellion will be formed. The strategy of integration can therefore be viewed as a gamble with high rewards and equally high risks. If it is successful, the payoff is highly rewarding; if it is unsuccessful, the result is likely to be disaster.

The British Policy: A Curious Amalgam

British policy toward Ireland in the centuries before the Union is accurately characterized as a strategy of coercion. Ireland was a colony whose land and people were ruthlessly exploited to serve British interests. British dominion, exercised by a minority of soldiers, settlers and administrators ruling over an alien and restless people, rested on the threat and actual application of force and terror. Settlers were encouraged to farm land expropriated from the indigenous inhabitants and were given arbitrary and absolute power over the lives and fortunes of the natives.

Although the British relied principally upon their preponderant military power to guarantee their authority in Ireland, after 1640 they employed the additional tactic of policies designed to prevent a native elite from developing. The Penal Laws, legislated after Cromwell's suppression of the Irish insurgents, forbade Irish Catholics to serve in the army, to enter politics, to own land or practice a profession, to import or export, to send their children to a Catholic school in Ireland or abroad for an education. Such repressive measures, coupled with a further expropriation of Irish lands (and even a policy of extermination), were consciously designed to reduce the wealth, power and organizational capabilities of the Irish people. Like eastern Europe, Ireland was to be reduced to a productive, untroublesome asset. The interests of the native inhabitants were entirely sacrificed to the interests of the metropolitan power.

In the first fifty years after the Union British policy toward Ireland became a curious amalgam of the two basic strategies that satisfied the conditions of neither but deepened the pitfalls of both. The avowed goal of successive British governments was the integration of the Irish people into the British nation. To some extent policies designed to achieve this goal were implemented. Discriminatory restrictions against Irish Catholics and the Catholic religion were largely removed. The Penal Laws had been struck down in the decades before the Union, and Catholic emancipation was granted several decades afterwards. The Catholic church was allowed to operate without legal interference and was even given some state support. The government allocated more funds for Irish education—both parochial and secular—and actively promoted job mobility within the civil service. The outlay for the development of roads and other transportation facilities, public health and social services also increased many-fold in the first fifty years of Union.

As a result, there was an increase in literacy and education, an increase in wealth (though not between 1830 and 1850) and a corresponding increase in the store of specialized technical and administrative skills among the Irish people. Although the Ireland of 1850 was still a predominantly agrarian country, the middle class, which had begun to emerge at the beginning of the century, had increased its size and solidified its power. An Irish intelligentsia had emerged that fully participated in the avant-garde political and artistic trends of the European intellectual elite.

There was the other side to the coin. Throughout this period the British continued to exploit Ireland. At the beginning of the century British industrialists had rigged the commercial clauses of the Union in such a way that they were easily able to destroy infant Irish industry and guarantee a large market in Ireland for finished British goods. British industrialists also exploited the chronic unemployment of Ireland by paying substandard wages to Irish workers imported from that island. The Protestant church continued to receive a substantial part of Irish revenues, even though it did little to contribute to the well-being or spiritual welfare of the majority of the Irish people. The Irish administration, although it became progressively more responsive to Irish interests after 1830, still included many individuals who viewed their jobs as mere sinecures or as rewards for past service. The British parliament continued to legislate differently for Ireland and England and refused to grant the Irish those basic civil liberties all Englishmen believed to be their natural inheritance. Above all, the Irish landed interests, through a notorious abuse of their arbitrary power, mercilessly exploited the Irish peasantry and contributed more than anyone else to the economic malaise of the countryside.

Exploitation and responsiveness were mutually exclusive. Therefore the reforms designed to meet the demands of the Irish people were unsuccessful in promoting reconciliation because they did not redress the core grievances arising from continuing exploitation and oppression. The Irish, for example, were given parliamentary representation, yet it proved ineffectual in guaranteeing the civil liberties of the Irish people. Irishmen were employed by the British administration in Ireland, but policy was still formulated by bureaucrats who were largely unresponsive to Irish needs. The Catholic church was made legal in Ireland and even subsidized by the state, but the established church continued to draw heavily on the Irish revenues. Reform, rather than satisfying Irishmen's demands, made the hopelessness of their position even more apparent and thus fanned the flames of their discontent.

The political, religious and economic reforms, coupled with the increasing British commitment of resources in Ireland, created conditions in which a middle class and native intelligentsia could develop. However, change and reform were not sufficiently far-reaching to fulfill the expectations of these classes for wealth, prestige, honor and equality. Aware of the possibilities for change, furious with the inequalities still remaining, and possessing technical and administrative skills and increasing capital, these classes mobilized the masses to support their demands and became the spearhead of the national movement. The Repeal movement, which had asked only for equality, was eclipsed by national movements like Young Ireland, the Fenians and Sinn Fein that demanded independence. In the end, it was the nationalist movement which secured the loyalty of the Irish people and successfully challenged British rule.

A Paradigm of Colonial History

The conclusions reached by Rupert Emerson in his impressive study *From Empire to Nation* suggest that the same contradictory dualism which characterized the Anglo-Irish relationship was a general feature of European colonial policy.[3] Emerson offers a paradigm of colonial history to explain the developmental sequence of colonial peoples from subject status to independence.

Emerson divides the colonial period in Asia and Africa into three stages, each representative of a distinct attitude manifested by the native population toward Western rule. According to him, the first period was characterized by a xenophobic rejection of colonial rule. The indigenous inhabitants, led by their traditional leaders, rose in rebellion against the alien invader. The colonial power's values, political forms and physical presence were violently rejected by the society. The Boxer rebellion, the Indian mutiny and the uprising of the Mahdi in the Sudan were all representative of this phase of interaction between the colonizer and the colonized. Such attempts to expel the foreigners and return to the traditional way of life were unsuccessful. The power of the traditional elite was frequently broken by the uprising, and often they retained a negligible influence only by reason of the grace accorded to them by the occupying nation. In such cases they proved useful as an administrative link between the colonial authorities and the native population. Over successive generations, this arrangement frequently proved fruitful to both parties, and the colonial power was able to retain the loyalties of this class until independence.

The second period was characterized by a swing from

xenophobic rejection to emulation. The change developed gradually, and only after radical alterations in the indigenous patterns of life had been effected by European occupation. A modern market economy developed alongside the precolonial subsistence economy. Urban centers, the loci of the European community, grew in size and importance and attracted natives from the hinterland. The cities were the centers of operation for overseas companies and the expanding colonial administration and were increasingly populated by a rising class of native entrepreneurs. As colonial governments and metropolitan commercial enterprises extended their operations, they found it necessary to introduce modern health services, to establish schools and to train elements of the native population in the skills and techniques of industrial society. This was partly a function of need and partly a response, Emerson argues, to growing pressures at home to improve the lot of the natives. Missionaries and charitable organizations tended the bodies and minds of natives as well as their souls.

Thus urbanization and the spread of literacy, the growth of secular education and the diffusion of technical and administrative skills among the native population were by-products of European colonial rule. These changes gave rise to a Europeanized element in the colony, concentrated in the urban centers and coexisting with the majority of the native population that remained rooted in its traditional ways. A new class of native had emerged. Fluent in the language of the colonizer, skilled in the techniques of the West and schooled in the ideas and values of European civilization, members of this new elite demanded the power, wealth and status accorded Europeans with similar qualifications. These *evolués*, as the French called them—often educated at Oxford, the Sorbonne or The Hague—rejected their old cultures and openly embraced the new. They considered themselves not so much Ibo, Arab or Malay as English, French or Dutch.

Some members of this first generation of culturally uprooted individuals were able to achieve high mobility in their adopted societies. This was especially evident in the

French colonies, where assimilation was the avowed policy of the government. Two examples are Félix Houphouet-Boigny of the Ivory Coast, who became a cabinet minister, and Léopold Senghor, a noted poet (in the French language) who was honored by membership in the prestigious French Academy. Such persons, however, represented a minority of the emerging native elite; most others like them were refused positions for which they believed their training and experience qualified them. Although competent and hard-working and honest in their adoption of European customs, they remained "natives" to the colonialists, who refused to bestow upon them the status freely granted less qualified members of the European community. In short, they remained frustrated in their attempt to achieve the benefits of the new order.

These frustrated Europeanized elements of the colony, Emerson argues, were not blind to the anomaly between word and deed. Colonial governments sought justification in the name of secular enlightenment and frequently articulated their "mission" as the diffusion of the benefits of Western civilization. To the colonial population this appeared to be sheer hypocrisy, as they saw themselves being denied these very benefits.

Bitterness in the face of such discrimination—justified by colonialists on the basis of racial or ethnic differences—was sharpened by the all-too-obvious contrast between this treatment and the ideas of equality and human dignity the elite had imbibed from their European education. The Declaration of the Rights of Man was a far cry from the realities of life in the colony. They also could not help but perceive the manner in which their fellow natives were treated as compared to the growing concern and solicitude shown the masses in Europe. As Europeans were achieving the rights of political participation and were being given the opportunity of deciding their own destinies, the colonial population was being denied these same rights. Two distinct political and administrative codes had developed, one for the European at home or in the colonies and another for the native. Governments quick to respond to the needs of their European citizens were blithely unresponsive to the demands of their colonial subjects. The result was that the Europeanized elements of the native population grew to believe that as long as colonial domination continued they and their fellows would remain in a subordinate status.

The reaction to this impasse led to the third and final stage of colonialism. The disillusioned *evolués* rejected assimilation into Western society in favor of assertion of their native culture. Emerson and others argue that colonial nationalism was an attempt by this elite to create a new environment, a new society in which they could achieve the power, wealth and status denied them by both the traditional and the Western societies. At the same time they were motivated by a concern to obtain justice, good government and economic well-being for the mass of the colonial population. Colonial nationalism was a synthesis of the two cultures: European rule was 'rejected, but not the attributes of Western power; the complacence and rigid hierarchy of traditional society were deprecated, but not its cultural achievements, its language and some of its other traditions. Nationalist leaders embraced the methods of the West in order to turn them against the colonial powers.

The native intelligentsia drew increasing support from other classes of society to whom nationalism also offered an attractive vehicle through which to satisfy their ambitions. Native professional men and entrepreneurs, civil servants and trade unionists—all drawn from the urbanized and culturally uprooted segment of society—swelled the ranks of the national movement. The money and organizational cadres necessary to mobilize the masses were drawn from these social groups. Frustrated by the contrast between their poverty and the wealth of the Europeans, and indignant over their lack of status in their own country, the masses were easily aroused by a movement that promised to raise their standard of living and confer upon them a new dignity.

If Emerson is correct, then the European colonial powers appear to have followed in Africa and Asia the same curious amalgam of the two strategies of colonialism that Britain pursued with regard to Ireland. On the one hand, the colony was exploited in order to provide raw materials, cheap labor, military conscripts and wider markets for Western capital and goods. To insure the success of these ventures, the native population was denied any share of real political power in the colony and deprived of much of its wealth. On the other hand, the policies of the colonial administrations gave rise to a small but articulate class of native entrepreneurs and intellectuals, skilled in the techniques of the West, familiar with the ideals of European society and demanding their share of the wealth, power and prestige.

In this connection it must be noted that the rise of such a class was not a necessary function of colonial rule. Certainly some natives had to be taught to read and had to be exposed to the techniques of Western society, but those Western powers that professed democratic values at home encouraged such development far beyond the mere requirements of administration in the colony. Education and enlightenment became goals in themselves. Students were sent to the great European universities, where they drank in the currents of egalitarian and radical thought. They returned home with an even greater awareness of the differences between their societies and European ones and with greater expectations as to their mobility, which, we have seen, remained unfulfilled. This proved to be a tremendous impetus to the development of national movements, for it increased the size of the cadres that would organize the movements. At the same time education and innovation within the colonies swelled the number of those who looked to these men for leadership. The proof that education fostered nationalism can be seen in the fact that those great colonial powers, such as Spain and Portugal, which made no pretext of bringing secular enlightenment to their colonies are the last to face the challenge of organized independence movements.

It was not difficult for colonial powers to admit a few *evolués* into their ranks. This required no radical restructuring of colonial society. When, however, greater numbers of natives began to demand similar privileges and opportunities, the colonial regimes were presented with a serious challenge. Like Britain in Ireland they were forced to make a choice between two alternative and mutually exclusive strategies. Like Britain in Ireland they appeared unable to do so and thus contributed to—if not caused—the rise of an alienated elite that challenged the basis of colonial authority.

The Stereotype Revisited

It is apparent from this analysis that the same irrational strategy pursued in Ireland was pursued in other colonial relationships as well. Could it be that the same perceptive myopia was the cause in these other cases?

In Ireland we have seen how a stereotyped image of the native was invented to justify colonial occupation. The stereotype functioned as a tension-reduction mechanism and, eventually, as a perceptual prison that blinded the British government to the reality of political and economic conditions in Ireland. As a result the British government initiated policies which were irrational in the sense that they fulfilled neither the goal of integration nor that of exploitation. What evidence is there of the existence of a similar perceptual blindness in other colonial situations?

Sensitive observers have provided us with ample evidence of stereotyped images of natives in almost all colonial situations. Descriptions of these stereotypes and commentary about their effects abound in both fictional and nonfictional studies of colonialism.

The original colonial novel, built on the theme of the Dutch experience in Indonesia, was probably *Max Havelaar*, first published in 1860.[4] The stereotypic qualities attributed to the Indonesian native hardly differed from those which characterized Paddy. With reference to the French colonial empire, the novels of Albert Memmi serve to illuminate the many striking parallels between the stereotypes of Irish and Algerians.[5] Similarly, ample evidence can be found in the English-speaking world. The theme of colonial stereotypes is at the core of George Orwell's *Burmese Days,* E. M. Forster's *Passage to India* and several of the novels of Graham Greene.[6] Forster provided a particularly insightful analysis of how such images served to solidify the colonial community and set the colonizer apart from the native. Forster and Orwell also stressed a perceptual gap created by the images, making meaningful communication between the worlds of colonizer and colonized all but impossible.

The stereotype of the Black American is another example. Its content and effects have been treated in novels like those of Mark Twain, Richard Wright and James Baldwin, and in serious academic investigations, the most impressive of which remains Gunnar Myrdal's *An American Dilemma.*[7]

The most fascinating aspect of the content of the stereotypes found in such works is that, while they describe such widely differing environments and peoples as those of Ireland and Indonesia, Algeria, Black America, Burma and Nigeria, the characteristics that colonizers attributed to the natives are remarkably uniform. With almost monotonous regularity colonial natives have been described as indolent and complacent, cowardly but brazenly rash, violent, uncivilized and incapable of hard work. On the more complimentary side, they have been characterized as hospitable, good-natured, possessing a natural talent for song and dance, and frequently as curious but incapable of a prolonged span of attention. In short, the image of simple creatures in need of paternal domination emerged very clearly. Each image, of course, varied slightly from the other, to include obvious differences in native character or mores, but the panoply of characteristics remained basically the same and effectively differentiated the natives from the white man.

Some observers have even suggested the function that the image of such characteristics fulfilled. Albert Memmi, in *The Colonizer and the Colonized,* commented on the utility of the belief that all natives are lazy. "It seems to receive unanimous approval," he wrote, "of colonizers from Liberia to Laos, via the Maghreb."

> It is easy to see to what extent this description is useful. It occupies an important place in the dialectics exalting the colonizer and humbling the colonized. Furthermore, it is economically fruitful. Nothing could better justify the colonizer's privileged position than his industry, and nothing could better justify the colonized's destitution than his indolence. The mythical portrait of the colonized therefore includes an unbelievable laziness, and that of the colonizer, a virtuous taste for action. At the same time the colonizer suggests that employing the colonized is not very profitable, thereby authorizing his unreasonable wages.[8]

The same might be and has in fact been said with reference to a series of other beliefs which functioned, as in the case of Ireland, to reduce tension and justify colonial policy. Jean Paul Sartre said in this connection:

> How can an elite of usurpers, aware of their mediocrity, establish their privileges? By one means only: debasing the colonized to exalt themselves, denying the title of humanity to the natives, and defining them as simply absences of qualities—animals, not humans. This does not prove hard to do, for the system deprives them of everything. Colonialist practice has engraved the colonialist idea into things themselves; it is the movement of things that designates colonizer and colonized alike. This oppression justifies itself through oppression: the oppressors produce and maintain by force the evils that render the oppressed, in their eyes, more and more like what they would have to be like to deserve their fate.[9]

Thus, Sartre concludes, colonial stereotypes become self-fulfilling and self-justifying images.

It is only natural to progress one step beyond this stage and examine the effect such images had upon policy. If the stereotypes were functional in reducing tension in other colonies besides Ireland, and if they dominated perception and became self-fulfilling—which evidence seems to suggest—then it is equally likely that as in the case of Ireland they became perceptual prisons through which colonial policy was evaluated and formulated. The existence of stereotyped images which distorted reality into harmony with the psychological needs of the colonizing society would explain not only the failure of colonial powers to perceive the necessity of choice between the two alternative strategies we have discussed, but also their inability to react rationally to the challenge of nationalist movements.

If the stereotype operated as a perceptual prison, then, as in Ireland, the characteristics attributed to the native population suggested the assumptions within which colonial policy was formulated. The most important of these assumptions were the following beliefs: (1) that the natives were incapable of self-government; (2) a corollary, that the native inhabitants were in need of the strong parental authority of the colonial power; (3) that colonial rule, therefore, was in the best interests of the native; and (4) another corollary, that the natives knew this.

The colonialists, of course, believed that the natives recognized the natural authority of the white man and were accordingly loyal to the colonial regime. These assumptions created the parameters for colonial policy. They limited the number and range of policy alternatives which were thought to be applicable to colonial administration. Policies outside the parameters set by the assumptions would be rejected, because accepting them would challenge the validity of the assumptions.

Rigid adherence to either the strategy of coercion or the strategy of integration involved policies which were beyond these parameters. On the one hand, the natives could not be ruled entirely by force and coercion and be denied all opportunities to partake of the wealth of the colony because this would clearly invalidate the colonialist's claim to have the best interests of the native in mind. On the other hand, promoting integration of the natives into the national community was equally unthinkable because they were perceived as being incapable of self-government and unable to cope with the privileges and responsibilities granted to the domestic population. The image of the native, therefore, dictated a colonial strategy halfway between the two basic alternatives.

Colonial powers professing to adhere to democratic values accordingly encouraged native education, introduced certain social services and provided some job mobility for talented colonials. At the same time their assumptions led them to deny the native any real exercise of political power or opportunity to achieve economic and social equality with the people of the colonizer's own nation. The colonial administration developed little empathy with the natives, could not perceive them as equals and was unable to accept their demands for equality as reasonable. Thus the native elite whose development was stimulated by colonial policies was also alienated by them. Increasingly it turned to nationalism as the solution to its dilemma.

The assumptions formulated in terms of the stereotyped image also provide an explanation for the irrational response of the colonial powers to native nationalism or protest. Once the colonial power was confronted with a rising protest movement, it had two practical alternatives to pursue: to accept the challenge and crush the movement, or to meet the demands of the native politicians in the hope of minimizing the appeal of nationalism and perhaps postponing or preventing the day when the leaders would demand total independence. But most colonial powers were unable to choose between these alternatives. Most of them could not perceive native political movements as a real threat because they remained convinced not only that independence was impossible, but that the vast majority of native inhabitants were content with their administration and were only being misled by agitators. The protest movements were accordingly explained away, as in Ireland, in terms of the ambitions of self-seeking, vicious agitators or deluded madmen. At the same time the colonial powers could not bring themselves to take action which would really have repressed such protest. Certainly leaders were jailed, meetings broken up and civil liberties partially suspended. The leaders were, however, usually released after short sentences; their supporters were repressed but not exterminated; censorship was imposed, but the nationalist presses were not smashed; and civil liberties were only temporarily suspended. In Ireland, for example, Daniel O'Connell was found guilty of treason by a rigged jury, but the decision was reversed by the House of Lords. The Young Ireland revolutionaries, captured after the rebellion of 1848, were not hanged but only temporarily deported, and the Irish press, which more than ever was agitating for independence, continued to indict the policies of the British government.

The histories of independence movements in India, Nigeria, Kenya, Algeria and Indonesia are not dissimilar. The values of the colonial administrators and the pressures exerted by public opinion at home generally prevented the reprisals and garrison-state tactics that characterized the policies of colonial powers like Portugal and Spain. Some pretense of democratic government had to be preserved if the colonizers were still to claim justification of their policies in terms of the model of colonial government they themselves had propagated.[10]

The colonialist response, therefore, usually consisted of a combination of mild repression and minor reform. Colonial administrators continued to believe that the protests of the natives were not really motivated by political concerns. They assumed that the masses neither understood nor wanted independence and the political machinery it entailed, and that their political aspirations were merely the result of passions inflamed by agitators seeking power.

Lord Lloyd, high commissioner of Egypt in the 1920s, whose attitude may be taken to be representative of the views of most colonial administrators, concluded:

Good administration is their [the natives'] only desire and concern—and it is because we have allowed administration to be
obscured by political issues that we have brought such heavy
troubles upon the shoulders of all concerned. In these countries
the real problem has been administrative, and we have chosen
to regard it as political.[11]

The proper focus of colonial rule, therefore, was to provide
peace and quiet from above so that the common people could
pursue their goals. Accordingly, greater attention was paid to
administrative than to political matters (although some minor
concessions were granted in the economic and political
spheres).

The result was to demonstrate to the people of the colony
that history was on the side of the nationalists. Though their
demands were still unmet, the political agitators were allowed
to continue operating. Their defiance of the colonial government with relative impunity from reprisal, and their partial
success in gaining concessions, strengthened their hand and
increased their power among the natives of the colony. In the
end the colonial government was presented with a real confrontation. Colonial powers were given the choice of granting
independence, as happened in India, Nigeria and French
Equatorial Africa, or of throwing overboard all pretext of
democracy and attempting to rule the colonies as occupied
countries, as happened in Indochina, Algeria and Ireland. By
the time the confrontation developed, however, the power of
the national movements had increased and the means necessary to preserve colonial rule had become so contradictory to
the values of a democratic society that there was fierce resis-
tance at home to the use of those means. These factors, coupled with the fact that the international balance of power favored the independence movements, sealed the fate of
widespread colonial empire.

In sum, the successful maintenance of colonial rule depended on rigid adherence to either of the two basic strategies. Halfway measures and compromise proved fatal to do-

minion. A choice had to be made. If the metropolitan power ruled the colonies as territories to be exploited at the expense of their inhabitants, it could not shrink from adopting coercive measures—inhumane as they may have appeared—if colonial authority was to be preserved. If, on the other hand, authority was to be maintained by securing the loyalty of the native population, the metropolitan power could not exploit the colony at the expense of its inhabitants. The colonizer had to develop empathy and accept the sacrifices required to legitimate the political connection.

Britain and France—the two primary examples of a democratic colonial power—were unable to commit themselves to either strategy. The majority of the political elites in both nations were unwilling to relinquish the advantages they believed metropolitan powers should derive from governing colonies and were unable to see independence as a practical alternative. At the same time, however, they viewed with increasing repugnance authority that rested entirely upon coercion. They were very reluctant to endorse the means required to preserve political power in the colonies. The problem can equally well be stated in reverse. As a result of the changing political climate of the nineteenth century Britain and France were compelled to legitimate their authority in the eyes of the colonial population but were unable or unwilling to make the sacrifices required by such a course of action.

As the century unfolded the dilemma grew more oppressive. In certain respects it reflected a basic paradox of the age. The nineteenth century was an era in which liberalism made great gains. The liberal ideology carried with it a commitment to government conducted in the interests of the majority of the people. Great emphasis was placed on the morality of political behavior. As liberalism outgrew its early doctrinaire tenets and incorporated ideas put forward by those concerned with social justice, an increasing emphasis was placed on improving the condition of the lower classes and extending spiritual and material welfare and the right of political participation to more and more people.

The nineteenth century was also an age in which political struggles were increasingly viewed in an ideological context. When the nation-state replaced the dynastic political unit and mass participation became a relevant factor, both the means and ends of political action underwent a significant change. Political differences and rivalries between nations tended to be defined in an ideological context in order to obtain from the population the sacrifices required to pursue foreign-policy goals. This was true of colonial rivalries as well as those in other areas. Colonization could be justified by the need to preclude takeover by a foreign power with a hostile ideology. And formerly unacceptable means and sacrifices were justified by the overriding importance of the ultimate goal.

Although colonial government was subject to increasing moral criticism, the nineteenth century will be remembered as the great age of Western colonial expansion. Colonies were perceived as vitally important sources of political and economic power in the struggle for the mastery of Europe. From 1870 to the end of the century, European penetration into colonial territories increased, as did the total territory effectively controlled by the metropolitan powers.

Many Europeans, especially those of a liberal persuasion, were forced to choose between their principles and what was regarded by them as political necessity. The majority of the liberals, seduced by arguments in favor of imperial expansion, envisaged colonial empire as a prerequisite to national power and even national survival. Somehow, principles and necessity had to be reconciled.

There was an additional dilemma at work as well. Because political rivalries had been structured in an ideological context, those persons who believed that their nation represented freedom and justice, as opposed to the tyranny of the rival, could not easily espouse political behavior—even if they thought it necessary—that contradicted the very goals for which the struggle was supposedly being waged. Englishmen who condemned French barbarities and undemocratic practices in Algeria could hardly admit that they pursued a similar policy in Ireland and India. The reverse held true, of course, for the French.

Thus the dilemma created by the conflict between the emerging value consensus of European democratic society and the means of political behavior in the colonies increased in intensity during the century. There can be little doubt that it produced a great psychological problem for the actors involved. Tension was generated that somehow had to be reduced. The means employed, this study has argued, was a perceptual sleight of hand, a stereotyped image of reality, which enabled those suffering from the dilemma to rationalize into harmony the contradiction between moral belief and political necessity. This solution had a profound effect on later policy. For while it proved useful in reducing tension, it did so at the expense of a realistic perception of colonial affairs. In the end its influence on policy proved disastrous and contributed to the collapse of colonial empire.

Notes

1. See Joseph Schumpeter, *Imperialism and Social Classes*, trans. Heinz Norden (New York, 1951).
2. Karl Deutsch et al., *Political Community and the North Atlantic Area* (Princeton, N.J., 1957), 21.
3. Rupert Emerson, *From Empire to Nation* (Cambridge, Mass., 1960).
4. Edward Douwes Dekker, *Max Havelaar, or The Coffee Sales of the Netherlands Trading Company*, trans. W. Siebenhaar (New York, 1927).
5. See Albert Memmi, *Portrait d'un juif l'impasse* (Paris, 1962), and *La statue de sel* (Paris, 1966).
6. George Orwell, *Burmese Days* (London, 1935); E. M. Forster, *A Passage to India* (New York, 1924). For Graham Greene's treatment of stereotypes see especially *The Heart of the Matter* (London, 1948).

7. See Richard Wright, *Native Son* (New York, 1940); James Baldwin, *Go Tell It on the Mountain* (New York, 1953) and *Notes of a Native Son* (Boston, 1962); Gunnar Myrdal et al., *An American Dilemma: The Negro Problem and Modern Democracy* (New York, 1962).

8. Albert Memmi, *The Colonizer and the Colonized* (New York, 1965), 79.

9. Quoted in Memmi, *The Colonizer and the Colonized*, xxvi.

10. *Ibid.*, passim.

11. Quoted in Emerson, *From Empire to Nation*, 38.

Bibliography

PRIMARY SOURCES

MANUSCRIPTS

British Museum, London

    Peel Papers
    Wellesley Papers

National Library of Ireland

    Graham Papers (microfilm); originals at Netherby, Longtown, Cumberland
    Monteagle Papers
    O'Connell Papers

Public Records Office, London

    Russell Papers

DIARIES, JOURNALS AND MEMOIRS

Brougham, Lord. *Life and Times.* 3 vols. Edinburgh: Blackwood and Sons, 1871.

Burgoyne, John. *Life and Correspondence of Field Marshal Sir John Burgoyne.* Ed. George Wrottesley. 2 vols. London: Richard Bentley, 1873.

Clarendon, Fourth Earl of. *Life and Letters of George William Frederick Villiers, the Fourth Earl of Clarendon.* Ed. Sir Herbert Eustace Maxwell. London: Edward Arnold, 1913.

Duffy, Charles Gavan. *My Life in Two Hemispheres.* London: T. F. Unwin, 1898.

———. *Thomas Davis: The Memoirs of an Irish Patriot.* London: Kegan Paul, Trench, Trübner, 1890.

Graham, James. *The Life and Letters of Sir James Graham.* Ed. C. S. Parker. 2 vols. London: John Murray, 1907.

Greville, Charles Cavendish Fulke. *Greville Memoirs, Part II: A Journal of the Reign of Queen Victoria from 1837–1852.* London: Longmans, Green, 1885.

Meagher, Thomas Francis. *Meagher of the Sword: Speeches of Thomas Francis Meagher in Ireland, 1846–1848.* Dublin: M. H. Gell and Son, 1916.

————. *Memoirs of General Thomas Francis Meagher.* Ed. Michael Cavanagh. Worcester, Mass.: Messenger Press, 1892.

Morison, Samuel Eliot. *The Life and Letters of Harrison Gray Otis, Federalist, 1765–1848.* Vol. I. Boston: Houghton Mifflin, 1913.

O'Connell, Daniel. *Correspondence of Daniel O'Connell, the Liberator, with Notices of His Life and Times.* Ed. W. J. Fitzpatrick. London: J. Murray, 1888.

O'Connell, John. *Recollections and Experiences During a Parliamentary Career from 1833 to 1848.* 2 vols. London: Bentley, 1849.

Peel, Robert. *Memoirs by the Right Hon. Sir Robert Peel.* 2 vols. London: John Murray, 1856–1857.

Russell, John. *Early Correspondence of Lord John Russell, 1808–1840.* Ed. Rollo Russell. 2 vols. London: T. F. Unwin, 1913.

————. *Later Correspondence of Lord John Russell, 1840–1878.* Ed. G. P. Gooch. 2 vols. London: Longmans, Green, 1925.

Sheil, Richard Lalor. *Memoirs of the Rt. Hon. Richard Lalor Sheil.* Ed. W. T. McCullagh. 2 vols. London: Hurst and Blackett, 1855.

Wilbraham, Roger. *Journal of Sir Roger Wilbraham.* Ed. Harold Spencer Scott. London: Royal Historical Society, 1902.

PARLIAMENTARY DEBATES

Hansard's Parliamentary Debates. Third Series. London, 1831–1850.

PARLIAMENTARY PAPERS

1843 (504), XXIV. *Report of the Commissioners Appointed to Take the Census of Ireland for the Year 1841.*

1845 (605), XIX, 1. *Report from Her Majesty's Commissioners of Inquiry into the State of the Law and Practice with Respect to the Occupation of Land in Ireland.*

1845 (606), XIX, 57; (616), XXI, 1; (657), XXI, 1. *Evidence Taken Before Her Majesty's Commissioners of Inquiry into the State of the Law and Practice with Respect to the Occupation of Land in Ireland.*

1845 (672), XXII, 1; (673), XXII, 225. *Appendix and Index to Above Inquiry.*

1846 (734), XXXVII. *Correspondence and Accounts Relating to the Different Occasions on Which Measures Were Taken for the Relief of the People Suffering from Scarcity in Ireland, Between 1822 and 1839.*

1851 (1400), L, 327. *Abstracts of the Census of Ireland, Taken in the Years 1841 and 1851.*

1853. *General Indexes to the Accounts and Papers, Reports of Commissioners, Estimates, Etc., 1801–52.* Reprinted by His Majesty's Stationery Office, 1938.

HISTORIES

Anderson, Christopher. *Historical Sketches of the Native Irish, and Their Descendants; Illustrative of Their Past and Present State, with Regard to Literature, Education, and Oral Instruction.* Edinburgh: Oliver and Boyd, 1830.

Angel, John. *A General History of Ireland.* 2 vols. Dublin, 1781.

Atwood, William. *The History, and Reasons, of the Dependency of Ireland upon the Imperial Crown of the Kingdom of England.* London: D. Brown and T. Leigh, 1698.

Barlow, Stephen. *The History of Ireland.* 2 vols. London: Sherwood, Neely and Jones, 1814.

Barrington, Jonah. *Rise and Fall of the Irish Nation.* Dublin: James Duffy, 1843.

Barron, William. *History of the Political Connection Between England and Ireland, from the Reign of Henry II to the Present Time.* London: T. Cadell, 1780.

Borlase, Edmund. *The History of the Execrable Irish Rebellion.* London, 1680.

Borohme the Younger, Brian (pseud.). *Ireland, as a Kingdom and a Colony; or A Historical, Political, and Military Sketch of Its State Previous to and Since the Invasion Under Henry the Second.* London: Dolman, 1843.

Burdy, Samuel. *The History of Ireland, from the Earliest Ages to the Union.* Edinburgh: Doig and Sterling, 1817.

Cambrensis, Giraldus. *The Irish Historie Composed and Written by Giraldus Cambrensis, and Translated into English . . . by John Hooker. . . .* (Written in 1188.) In Raphael Holinshed et al., *The First and Second Volumes of Chronicles.* . . . Vol. II. London, 1577.

Camden, William. *Britannia, sine florentissimorum regnorum angliae, scotiae, hiberniae, et insularum adjacentium.* . . . London, 1586. The first English edition appeared in 1610.

Campion, Edmund. *A Historie of Ireland, Written in the Yeare 1571.* Dublin: Society of Stationers, 1633. Reprinted at Hibernia Press, 1809.

Canning, Albert S. G. *Revolted Ireland, 1798 and 1803.* London: W. H. Allen, 1886.

Carew, George. *Pacata Hibernia.* London, 1663.

Carey, Mathew. *Vindiciae Hibernicae; or, Ireland Vindicated. An Attempt to . . . Expose . . . the Multifarious Errors and Misrepresentations Respecting Ireland in the Histories of Macauley* (sic), *Hume and Others.* Philadelphia: H. C. Carey and I. Lea, 1823.

Comerford, Thomas. *The History of Ireland from the Earliest Account of Time, to the Invasion of the English Under King Henry II.* Dublin: E. Rider, 1754.

Coote, Charles. *History of the Union of the Kingdom of Great-Britain and Ireland; With an Introductory Survey of Hibernian Affairs, Traced from the Times of Celtic Colonisation.* London: S. Hamilton, 1802.

Corner, Julia. *The History of Ireland: From the Earliest Period to the Present Time* (adapted for youth, schools and families). London: T. Dean and Son, 1840.

Cox, Richard. *Hibernia anglicana.* 2 vols. London: J. Watts, 1689–1690.

Crawford, William. *A History of Ireland.* 2 vols. London: J. Bellew, 1783.

Crouch, Nathaniel. *The History of the Kingdom of Ireland.* . . . London, 1693.

Curry, John. *A Brief Account from the Most Authentic Protestant Writers Etc. of the Irish Rebellion of 1641.* London, 1747.

————. *An Historical and Critical Review of the Civil Wars in Ireland, from the Reign of Queen Elizabeth, to the Settlement Under King William.* . . . Dublin: R. Conolly, 1810. First published in 1775.

Davies, John. *A Discoverie of the State of Ireland: With the True Causes Why That Kingdom Was Never Entirely Subdued.* . . . (Written in 1613.) In *A*

Collection of Tracts and Treatises . . . of the State of Ireland. . . . London: John Stockdale, 1786.

Derricke, John. *The Image of Ireland.* London, 1581.

Faulkiner, Caesar L. *Illustrations of Irish Destiny and Topography, Mainly of the Seventeenth Century.* London: Longmans, Green, 1904.

Godwin, William. *History of the Commonwealth of England.* 4 vols. London, 1824–1828.

Gordon, J. Bentley. *A History of Ireland from the Earliest Accounts to the Accomplishment of the Union with Great Britain in 1801.* Dublin, 1805.

Harris, Walter. "An Essay on the Defects in the Histories of Ireland, and, Remedies Proposed for the Amendment and Reformation Thereof: in a Letter to the Right Honourable Robert, Lord Baron Newport of Newport, Lord Chancellor of Ireland. . . ." In Walter Harris, ed., *Hibernica.* Dublin: W. Harris, 1747.

Howell, James. *Divers Historical Discourses on the Late Popular Insurrection in Great Britain and Ireland.* London, 1661.

Hume, David. *History of England.* 8 vols. London: T. Cadell, 1778.

Hyde, Edward (Earl of Clarendon). *History of the Rebellion and Civil Wars in England.* Oxford, 1702.

Keane, John Henry. *The Substance of Three Lectures on the History of Ireland.* London: T. Jones, 1839.

Keating, Geoffrey. *A Complete History of Ireland from the First Colonisation of the Island by Parthalon to the Anglo-Norman Invasion.* Dublin, 1811.

Kelso, John J. *The Plantation of Ireland, or A Review of the Origin and History of Her Earlier Colonial Settlements.* Belfast: Archer and Sons, 1865.

Lawless, John. *A Compendium of the History of Ireland from the Earliest Period to the Reign of George I.* Dublin, 1814.

Ledwich, Edward. *The Antiquities of Ireland.* Dublin, 1790.

Leland, Thomas. *The History of Ireland from the Invasion of Henry II.* 3 vols. Dublin, 1773.

Lynch, John. *Cambrensis eversus.* Ed. and trans. Matthew Kelly. (Written in 1662.) 3 vols. Dublin, 1848–1850.

Lynch, Patrick. *The Life of St. Patrick.* Dublin, 1810.

Macaulay, Thomas Babington. *The History of England from the Accession of James II.* 5 vols. London, 1884.

McDermot, Martin. *A New and Important History of Ireland, from the Earliest Accounts to the Present Time.* London: J. M. M'Gowan, for G. Cowil, 1820–1823.

Mac-Geoghegan, James. *The History of Ireland, Ancient and Modern; Taken from the Most Authentic Records, and Dedicated to the Irish Brigade.* Trans. from the French by Patrick O'Kelly. Dublin: J. Duffy, 1844.

Martin, Robert Montgomery. *Ireland Before and After the Union with Great Britain.* London: W. S. Orr, 1843.

Martineau, Harriet. *History of England,* A.D. *1800–1815: Being an Introduction to the History of the Peace.* London: G. Bell and Sons, 1878.

Maxwell, Constantia. *Irish History from Contemporary Sources, 1509–1610.* London: G. Allen and Unwin, 1923.

———. *The Stranger in Ireland from the Reign of Elizabeth to the Great Famine.* London: Jonathan Cape, 1954.

Moore, Thomas. *The History of Ireland.* 3 vols. London: Longman, Brown, Green and Longman, 1835–1846.

Moryson, Fynes. *An History of Ireland from 1599 to 1603.* (Written circa 1617.) 2 vols. Dublin, 1735.

O'Conor, Charles. *Dissertations on the Antient History of Ireland: Wherein an Account Is Given of the Origine, Government, Letters, Sciences, Religion, Manners and Customs of the Antient Inhabitants. . . .* Dublin: M. Reilly, 1753.

———. *Rerum hibernicarum scriptores veteres.* 4 vols. Dublin, 1814–1826.

O'Conor, Matthew. *The History of the Irish Catholics.* Dublin, 1813.

O'Driscol, John. *The History of Ireland.* 2 vols. London: Longman, Rees, Orme, Brown, and Green, 1827.

O'Flaherty, Roderic. *Ogygia, or, A Chronological Account of Irish Events: Collected from Very Ancient Documents, Faithfully Compared with Each Other, and Supported by the Genealogical and Chronological Aid of the Sacred and Prophane Writings of the First Nations of the Globe.* Trans. from the Latin by Rev. James Hely. 2 vols. Dublin: W. M'Kenzie, 1793.

O'Halloran, Sylvester. *An Introduction to the Study of the History and Antiquities of Ireland: In Which the Assertions of Mr. Hume and Other Writers Are Occasionally Considered.* London: J. Murray, 1772.

Parnell, William. *An Historical Apology for the Irish Catholics in the Year, 1641.* Dublin, 1758.

Plowden, Francis P. *An Historical Review of the State of Ireland from the Invasion of That Country Under Henry II to Its Union with Great Britain.* 5 vols. London: F. C. and J. Rivington, 1803.

Regan, Maurice. "A Fragment of the History of Ireland by M. Regan." Trans. G. Carew. In Walter Harris, ed., *Hibernica.* Dublin: W. Harris, 1747.

Reily, Hugh. *Genuine History of Ireland . . . Since the Reformation.* Rev. ed. Boston: P. Mooney, 1838.

Shirley, James. *True Impartial History and Wars of the Kingdom of Ireland.* London, 1692.

Smiles, Samuel. *History of Ireland and the Irish People, Under the Government of England.* London: W. Strange, 1844.

Smith, Goldwin. *Irish History and Irish Character.* London: J. H. and J. Parker, 1862.

———. *Irish History and the Irish Question.* New York: McClure, Phillips, 1905.

Smyth, George Lewis. *Ireland: Historical and Statistical.* 3 vols. London: Whittaker, 1844–1849.

Story, George Warter. *An Impartial History of the War of Ireland.* London, 1693.

Taafe, Dennis. *An Impartial History of Ireland, from the Period of the English Invasion to 1810.* 4 vols. Dublin: J. Christie, 1809–1811.

Temple, John. *The Irish Rebellion; or, An History of the Attempts of the Irish Papists to Extirpate the Protestants in the Kingdom of Ireland; Together with the Cruelties and . . . Massacres Which Ensued Thereupon.* London: J. Brindley, 1746.

Vitus, S. (Stephen White). *Apologia pro Hibernia adversus cambri calumnias.* Ed. Matthew Kelly. (Written circa 1615.) Dublin, 1849.

Waring, T. E. *A Brief Narrative of the Plotting, Beginning and Carrying On of That Execrable Rebellion and Butcherie in Ireland.* London, 1649.

Warner, Ferdinando. *The History of Ireland.* London: J. and R. Tonson, 1763.

Webb, William. *An Analysis of the History and Antiquities of Ireland.* Dublin, 1791.

Williams, Edwin. *A Political History of Ireland, Showing Its Connexion with England, from the Anglo-Norman Conquest, in 1172, by Henry II, to the Present Time.* New York: R. P. Bixly, 1843.

Wood, Thomas. *An Inquiry Concerning the Primitive Inhabitants of Ireland.* London: printed for G. and N. W. Whittaker, 1821.

Wynne, John H. *A General History of Ireland . . . to the Death of King William III.* London: G. Riley, 1773.

PAMPHLETS AND OTHER CONTEMPORARY PUBLICATIONS

Agricola (pseud.). *Suggestions on the Best Modes of Employing the Irish Peasantry, as an Anti-Famine Precaution.* London: J. Hatchard and Son, 1845.

Anketel, W. R. *The Effects of Absenteeism Briefly Considered. . . .* London: J. Hatchard and Son, 1843.

Anonymous. *An Abstract of the Unnatural Rebellion, and Barbarous Massacre of the Protestants, in the Kingdom of Ireland.* London: Richard Janeway, 1689.

————. *An Address to the Conservative Members of Parliament on the Present State of Affairs in Ireland.* Dublin: Grant and Bolton, 1845.

————. *The Alarm; or, The Irish Spy. In a Series of Letters on the Present State of Affairs in Ireland, to a Lord, High in the Opposition. Written by an Ex-Jesuit.* London: J. Bew, 1779.

————. *Cause of the Evils Existing in Ireland; with a Plain and Simple Remedy. . . . By One of the People.* London: T. R. Drury, 1834.

————. *Common Sense Against Repeal. By a Milesian.* Dublin: W. Curry, Jr., 1844. Nos. 1–18 (July 6–December 28).

————. *Considerations on the Present State of Ireland and on the Best Means of Improving the Condition of Its Inhabitants.* London: R. and A. Taylor, 1822.

————. *Emigration, a More Humane and More Profitable Test of Destitution Than the Workhouse, and Remarks on the Policy of Ministers with Respect to the Present Condition of Ireland, with Suggestions for Its Improvement.* London: Effingham Wilson, 1847.

————. *Essay on the Present State of Manners and Education Among the Lower Class of the People in Ireland.* 3rd ed. Dublin, 1805.

————. *How Is Ireland to Be Governed?* London: T. Jones, 1844.

————. "Incumbered Estates Court." *Dublin University Magazine,* XXXVI (September 1850), 311–328.

————. *Observations on the Habits of the Labouring Classes in Ireland. Suggested by Mr. C. C. Lewis' Report on the State of the Irish Poor in Great Britain.* Dublin: Milliken and Son, 1836.

————. *Observations on the Mutiny Bill: With Some Strictures on Lord Buckinghamshire's Administration in Ireland.* London: J. Stockdale, 1781.

————. *Relief to Ireland, Under the Recent Calamity, Out of the General Funds of the State, No Favour But a Matter of Right, by Nature of the Union.* Dublin: James McGlashan, 1847.

————. "Remarks on Some of the Evils of Ireland, and Their Removal. By a Protestant Inhabitant of the Province of Ulster." *The Pamphleteer*, XXV (1825).

————. *The Saying of Sir Robert Peel, "My Chief Difficulty Is Ireland," Considered and a Few Remedial Measures of That Country Considered. . . . By a Clergyman of the Arch-diocese of Canterbury.* London: John Ollivier, 1841.

————. *Thoughts on Ireland.* London: James Ridgway, 1847.

————. *What Science Is Saying About Ireland.* 2d ed. Kingston-upon-Hull: Leng and Co., 1882.

Arden, William (Lord Alvanley). *The State of Ireland Considered and Measures Proposed for Restoring Tranquillity to That Country.* London: John Ollivier, 1841.

Balfour, Arthur James. *Nationality and Home Rule.* London: Longmans, Green, 1913.

Ball, Charles. *An Union Neither Necessary or Expedient for Ireland?* Dublin: William Potter, 1798.

Battersby, W. J. *The Fall and Rise of Ireland, or the Repealer's Manual.* 2d ed. with supp. Dublin: T. O'Flanagan, 1834.

Beaumont, Gustave de. *L'Irlande sociale, politique et religieuse.* 2 vols. Paris: Librairie de C. Gosselin, 1839.

Bell, Robert. *A Description of the Condition and Manners as Well as of the Moral and Political Character, and Education, of the Peasantry of Ireland Such as They Were Between the Years 1780 and 1790, When Ireland Was Supposed to Have Arrived at Its Highest Degree of Prosperity and Happiness.* London: Charles Barber, 1804.

Bish, Thomas. *A Plea for Ireland in a Letter to the Right Hon. Lord Althorp.* London: J. M. Richardson, Cornhill, 1834.

Blacker, William. *Prize Essay, Addressed to the Agricultural Committee of the Royal Dublin Society; on the Management of Landed Property in Ireland.* Dublin, 1834.

Bridges, William. *Plantation of Ireland. Three Practical Suggestions for the Colonization and Re-organization of Ireland.* London: H. Bacclière, 1849.

Browne, Denis. *A Letter from the Right Hon. Denis Browne, M.P. for Kilkenny, to the Most Noble the Marquis Wellesley on the Present State of Ireland.* London: J. Nichols and Son, 1822.

Burke, Edmund. *Two Speeches on Conciliation with America, and Two Letters on Irish Questions.* London: G. Routledge and Son, 1886.

Burritt, Elihu. *A Journal of a Visit of Three Days to Skibereen, and Its Neighborhood.* London: Charles Gilpin, 1847.

Butt, Isaac. *Repeal of the Union: The Substance of a Speech Delivered in the Corporation of Dublin . . . 1843. . . .* Dublin: W. Curry, Jr., 1843.

Campbell, James. *Ireland, As It Was, Is, and Must Still Be, If Under the Tutelage of Jesuits, and as Lord Alvaney Proposes, the Paternal Rule of the Infallible Head of . . . the Pope.* Douglas, Isle of Man: William Dillon, 1842.

Campbell, Thomas. *A Philosophical Survey of the South of Ireland, in a Series of Letters to John Watkinson, M.P.* Dublin: printed for W. Whitestone, M.P., 1778.

Cavour, Camillo Benso. *Thoughts on Ireland: Its Present and Its Future.* Trans. W. B. Hodgson. London: Trübner, 1868.

Churton, Edward. *Sir Robert Peel, the Greatest Radical of the Age and the Best Friend of O'Connel* (sic). London: Edward Churton, 1845.

Cobden, Richard. *England, Ireland and America.* London: P. Brown, 1836.

Colquhoun, J. C. *Ireland; Popery and Priestcraft the Cause of Her Misery and Crime. Sponsored by the Glasgow Protestant Association.* Glasgow: William Collins, 1836.

Connor, William. *Two Letters to the Editor of The Times, on the Rackrent Oppression of Ireland, Its Source—Its Evils—and Its Remedy, in Reply to The Times Commissioner.* Dublin: Samuel J. Machen, 1846.

Cooke, David M. *The Irish Bench and British Constitution or, Cooke on O'Connell's Last Political Villainy.* Dublin, 1834.

Cooke, Henry. *Authentic Report of the Speech of . . . at the Great Protestant Meeting, Hillsborough.* Belfast: Stuart and Gregg, 1834.

Daunt, William Joseph O'Neill. *Ireland and Her Agitators.* Dublin: J. Browne, 1845.

Davis, John. *A Discoverie of the State of Ireland: With the True Causes Why That Kingdom Was Never Entirely Subdued.* London: printed for John Jaggard, 1613.

Davison, John. *Considerations on the Justice and Wisdom of Conciliatory Measures Towards Ireland.* Oxford: W. Baxter, 1829.

De Vere, Aubrey Thomas. *English Misrule and Irish Misdeeds. Four Letters from Ireland Addressed to an English Member of Parliament.* London: J. Murray, 1848.

Devon, Lord. *Letter from an Irish Proprietor to the Ministers of Religion of the District.* London: J. Biggs and Son, 1847.

Dewar, Daniel. *Observations on the Character, Customs, and Superstitions of the Irish, and on Some of the Causes Which Have Retarded the Moral and Political Improvement of Ireland.* London: Cole and Curtis, 1812.

De Witte, G. J. *Financial Plan for the Relief of Ireland and the Landlords of Ireland.* London: Saunders and Otley, 1847.

Dicey, Albert Venn. *England's Case Against Home Rule.* London: J. Murray, 1886.

Doyle, James Warren. *Letters on the State of Ireland.* Dublin: R. Coyne, 1825.

Edgeworth, Maria. *The Absentee.* New York: Dodd, Mead, 1893.

Ensor, George. *Observations on the Present State of Ireland.* Dublin: H. Fitzpatrick, 1814.

Fagan, Michael Joseph. *The Repeal of the Union Would Be Separation.* . . . Dublin: S. J. Machen, 1841.

Fairplay, Frank (pseud.). *The Repeal of the Union Between Great Britain and Ireland, Compared with the Separation of Belgium and Holland.* London: J. M. Richardson, 1831.

Firth, William. "The Case of Ireland Set at Rest: A Letter to the Rt. Hon. Robert Peel, M.P." *The Pamphleteer,* XXV (1825), 162–182.

Freeman, Edward A. *Lectures to American Audiences.* Philadelphia: Porter and Coates, 1882.

––––––. *Some Impressions of the United States.* London: Longmans, 1883.

Gilly, W. S., ed. *Ireland: Letters from a Lady.* Durham: G. Andrews, 1847.

Godley, John Robert. *Observations on the Irish Poor Law.* Dublin: Grant and Bolton, 1847.

Goold, Henry. *Thoughts on a Judicious Disposition of Land in Ireland. . . .* London: Effingham Wilson, 1847.

Gore, Montague. *Suggestions for the Amelioration of the Present Condition of Ireland.* London: James Ridgway, 1847.

Grant, James. *Impressions of Ireland and the Irish.* 2 vols. London: H. Cunningham, 1844.

Gray, John. *A Plan for Finally Settling the Government of Ireland upon Constitutional Principles; and the Chief Cause of the Unprosperous State of That Country Explained.* London: printed for J. Stockdale, 1785.

Harcourt, Daniel. *A New Remonstrance from Ireland Containing an Exact Declaration of the Cruelties, Insolencies, Outrage, and Murders Exercised by the Bloudthirsty, Popish Rebells in That Kingdome upon Many Hundred Protestants in the Province of Ulster . . . since . . . 1641.* London: H. Shephard, 1643.

Hassard, Richard Major. *Popery, as It Is, and Will Be, Until Destroyed. . . .* Dublin: Grant and Bolton, 1839.

Hibernicus (pseud.). *Practical Views and Suggestions on the Present Condition and Permanent Improvement of Ireland.* Dublin: J. Carrick and Son, 1823.

Hillary, William. "A Sketch of Ireland in 1824: The Sources of Her Evils Considered, and Their Remedies Suggested." *The Pamphleteer,* XXV (1825), 1–18.

Hogan, Edmund. *The Description of Ireland, and the State Thereof as It Is at This Present in Anno 1598.* Dublin: M. H. Gill and Son, 1878.

Horton, Robert John Wilmot. *Ireland and Canada; Supported by Local Evidence.* London, 1839.

Kennedy, John Pitt. *Instruct; Employ; Don't Hang Them; or, Ireland Tranquilized Without Soldiers, and Enriched Without English Capital.* London: T. and W. Boone, 1835.

Knox, Alexander. *Considerations on the State of Ireland.* Dublin: W. Watson, 1778.

——. *Essays on the Political Circumstances of Ireland.* Dublin: Graisberry and Campbell, 1798.

Macaulay, Thomas Babington. *Repeal of the Union with Ireland: A Speech . . . Delivered in the House of Commons. . . .* Dublin: Irish Loyal and Patriotic Union, 1886.

MacDonnell, Eneas. *Irish Sufferers and Anti-Irish Philosophers.* London: John Ollivier, 1847.

————. *Repeal of the Union; Letter in Opposition to That Measure.* London: Wilsher and Pite, 1833.

Madden, Daniel Owen. *The Impolicy and Injustice of Imprisoning O'Connell Demonstrated to Sir Robert Peel.* London: T. C. Newly, 1844.

Martineau, Harriet. *Ireland: A Tale.* London: C. Fox, 1832.

Maxwell, Constantia Elizabeth. *The Foundations of Modern Ireland; Select Extracts from Sources Illustrating English Rule and Social and Economic Conditions in Ireland in the Sixteenth and Early Seventeenth Century.* New York: Macmillan, 1921.

Meagher, Thomas Francis. *Speeches on the Legislative Independence of Ireland.* New York: Redfield, 1853.

Meekins, Robert. *Plan for the Removal of Pauperism, Agrarian Disturbance, and the Poor Rate in Ireland, by Liberally Providing for the Destitute Free of Expence.* Dublin: James McGlashen, 1847.

Meylar, Anthony. *Six Letters Addressed to Lord Stanley on the Political and Religious Condition of Ireland. . . .* Dublin: William Carson, 1841.

Mill, John Stuart. *England and Ireland.* London: Longmans, Green, Reader, and Dyer, 1868.

————. *Principles of Political Economy with Some of Their Applications to Social Philosophy.* 2 vols. Boston, 1848.

Milner, John. *An Inquiry into Certain Vulgar Opinions Concerning the Catholic Inhabitants and the Antiquities of Ireland, in a Series of Letters Addressed from That Island to a Protestant Gentleman in England.* 2d ed., rev. London: Keating, Brown, 1809(?).

Molyneux, William. *The Case of Ireland Being Bound by Acts of Parliament in England.* London: J. Almon, 1760.

Montgomery, H. *Letter from the Rev. H. Montgomery to Daniel O'Connell, Esq., M.P.* Dublin: W. Underwood, 1831.

Mornington, William (Viscount Wellesley). *The Irish Question Considered in Its Integrity.* Dublin: W. Curry, Jr., 1844.

Musgrave, Richard. *Strictures upon an Historical Review of the State of Ireland, by Francis Plowden . . . or, A Justification of the Conduct of the English Governments in That Country from the Reign of Henry the Second to the Union of Great Britain and Ireland.* London: F. C. and J. Rivington, 1804.

O'Donohue, P. *Irish Wrongs and English Misrule; or, The Repealer's Epitome of Grievances.* Dublin: A. C. Baynes, 1845.

Page, James. *Ireland: Its Evils Traced to Their Source.* London: R. B. Seeley and W. Burnside, 1836.

Parnell, William. *An Historical Apology for the Irish Catholics.* 2d ed. Dublin: H. Fitzpatrick, 1807.

Petty, William. "Political Anatomy of Ireland." In *A Collection of Tracts and Treaties of the State of Ireland.* 2 vols. (Originally published in 1691.) Dublin, 1861.

Plunkett, Edward. *Address to the Landowners of Ireland upon the Present Agitation for a Repeal of the Union.* London: J. Ridgway, 1843.

Price, Rose Lambart. *Ireland: A Satire.* 2d ed. London: J. and H. L. Hunt, 1824.

Ricardo, David. *The Works and Correspondence of David Ricardo.* Ed. Piero Sraffa with M. H. Dobb. 10 vols. Cambridge: Cambridge University Press, 1951–1955.

Roden, Earl of. *Observations on Lord Alvanley's Pamphlet on the State of Ireland . . . by the Earl of Roden.* London: J. Hatchard and Son, 1841.

Rogers, Jasper W. *Employment of the Irish Peasantry the Best Means to Prevent the Drain of Gold from England.* London: Trelawney Wm. Saunders, 1847.

————. *Facts for the Kind-Hearted of England as to the Wretchedness of the Irish Peasantry, and the Means for Their Regeneration.* London: James Ridgway, 1847.

————. *Letter to the Landlords and Ratepayers of Ireland, Relating to the Means for the Permanent and Profitable Employment of the Peasantry.* London: James Ridgway, 1846.

————. *The Potato Truck System of Ireland, the Main Cause of Her Periodical Famines and of the Non-Payment of Her Rents.* London: James Ridgway, 1849.

Rosse, Earl of. *Letters on the State of Ireland.* London: J. Hatchard and Son, 1847.

Ryan, John. *A Letter to the Protestants of Ireland (Sponsored by the Protestant Union).* Dublin: William Curry, Jr., 1844.

Sadler, Michael Thomas. *Ireland: Its Evils and Their Remedies, Being a Reflection of the Errors of the Emigration Committee and Others, Touching That Country.* London: J. Murray, 1829.

Scrope, George Poulett Thomason. *How Is Ireland to Be Governed?* London: Ridgway and Son, 1834.

——. *The Irish Poor Law: How Far Has It Failed and Why?* London: James Ridgway, 1849.

——. *Letters to Lord John Russell, M.P., on the Further Measures Required for the Social Amelioration of Ireland.* London: James Ridgway, 1847.

——. *Plan of a Poor-Law for Ireland, with a Review of the Arguments For and Against It.* London, 1833.

Senior, Nassau William. *Journals, Conversations and Essays Relating to Ireland.* 2 vols. London: Longmans, Green, 1868.

Shrewsbury, Earl of (John Talbot). *Hints Towards the Pacification of Ireland: Addressed More Particularly to the Ruling Powers of the Day.* London: C. Dolman, 1844.

——. *A Second Letter to Ambrose Lisle Phillips, Esq., from the Earl of Shrewsbury on the Present Posture of Affairs.* London: Charles Dolman, 1841.

Spenser, Edmund. *A View of the State of Ireland.* . . . London: James Ware, 1633.

——. "A View of the State of Ireland." In *The Works of That Famous English Poet, Mr. Edmund Spenser.* London: printed by Henry Hills for Jonathan Edwin, 1679.

Stanley, William. *Commentaries on Ireland.* Dublin: R. Millikin and Son, 1833.

Stapleton, Augustus Granville. *The Real Monster Evil of Ireland.* London: J. Hatchard and Son, 1843.

——. *Sequel to the Real Monster Evil of Ireland.* London: J. Hatchard and Son, 1843.

Staunton, Michael. *Reasons for a Repeal of the Legislative Union Between Great Britain and Ireland.* Dublin: J. Duffy, 1845.

Swift, Jonathan. *The Drapier's Letters to the People of Ireland.* Ed. Herbert Davis. Oxford: Oxford University Press, 1935.

————. *The Irish Writings of Jonathan Swift.* Ed. Oliver Watson Ferguson. Urbana: University of Illinois Press, 1954.

Taafe, Nicholas. *Observations on Affairs in Ireland from the Settlement in 1691 to the Present.* London: W. Griffin, 1766.

Tennent, James Emerson. *Speech of . . . on Seconding the Amendment of the Right Hon. T. Spring Rice, to Mr. O'Connell's Motion Relative to the Repeal of the Union, on the 22nd of April, 1834.* London: Edward Moxon, 1834.

Torrens, R. *Self-Supporting Colonization. Ireland Supported Without Cost to the Imperial Treasury.* London: James Ridgway, 1847.

Trevelyan, Charles. *Mr. Trevelyan on Ireland.* London: Irish Loyal and Patriotic Union, 1883.

————. *Three Letters to The Times on London Pauperism. . . .* London: Longmans, Green, 1870.

Tucker, Josiah. *Reflections on the Present Matters in Dispute Between Great Britain and Ireland.* London: T. Cadell, 1785.

Ward, James. *Remedies for Ireland. A Letter to the Right Hon. Lord Monteagle, on the Fallacy of the Proposed Poor Law, Emigration, and Reclamation of Waste Lands, as Remedies: Being a Postscript to "How to Reconstruct the Industrial Condition of Ireland."* London: Smith, Elder, 1847.

Williams, Charles Wye. *Observations on an Important Feature in the State of Ireland and the Want of Employment of Its Population. . . .* London: T. Vacher, 1831.

TRAVEL AND DESCRIPTIONS OF IRELAND

Barrow, John. *A Tour Round Ireland.* London: John Murray, 1836.

Bigelow, Andrew. *Leaves from a Journal of Sketches of Rambles in North Britain and Ireland.* Edinburgh: Oliver and Boyd, 1824.

Binns, Jonathan. *The Miseries and Beauties of Ireland.* 2 vols. London: Longman, Orme, Brown, 1837.

Buckley, James. "A Tour in Ireland in 1672–74." *Journal of the Cork Historical and Archaeological Society,* ser. 2, X (1904), 85–100.

Bush, John. *Hibernia Curiosa. A Letter from a Gentleman in Dublin, to His Friend at Dover in Kent, Giving a General View of the Manners, Customs, Dispositions, Etc. of the Inhabitants of Ireland.* London: W. Fleseney, 1768.

Carlyle, Thomas. *Reminiscences of My Irish Journey in 1849.* London: Sampson, Low, Marston, Searle and Rivington, 1882.

Carr, John. *The Stranger in Ireland: or, A Tour in the Southern and Western Parts of That Country in the Year 1805.* Philadelphia: T. and G. Palmer, 1806.

Chatterton, Henrietta G. *Rambles in the South of Ireland.* 2 vols. London: Saunders and Olley, 1839.

Clarke, Edward Daniel. *A Tour Through the South of England, Wales, and Parts of Ireland, Made During the Summer of 1791.* London: Minerva Press, 1793.

Cooper, George. *Letters on the Irish Nation, Written During a Visit to That Kingdom, in the Autumn of the Year 1799.* London: printed by J. Davis for J. White, 1800.

Croker, Thomas Crofton. *Researches in the South of Ireland.* London: J. Murray, 1824.

de Laboullaye le Gouz, François. *The Tour of the French Traveller M. de Laboullaye le Gouz in Ireland.* Ed. T. Crofton Croker. London: T. and W. Boone, 1837.

Derricke, John. *The Image of Irelande, with a Discoverie of Wood-karne.* (Originally published in 1581.) Edinburgh: A. and C. Black, 1883.

de Tocqueville, Alexis. *Journeys to England and Ireland.* Ed. J. P. Mayer. New York: Doubleday, 1968.

Dingley, James. "Observations in a Voyage Through the Kingdom of Ireland . . . in the Year 1681." *The Journal of the Kilkenny and South East of Ireland Archaeological Society* (Dublin), 1870.

Edgcumbe, Richard. "The Voyage of Sir Richard Edegcomb [sic] into Ireland, in the Year 1488." In Walter Harris, ed., *Hibernica.* Dublin: W. Harris, 1747.

Hall, James. *Tour Through Ireland; Particularly the Interior and Least Known Parts: Containing an Accurate View of the Parties, Politics, and Improvements, in the Different Provinces.* 2 vols. London: R. P. Moore, 1813.

Hall, Samuel Carter, and A. M. F. Hall. *Ireland: Its Scenery, Character, Etc.* 2d ed. 3 vols. London: J. How, 1846.

Hoare, Richard Colt. *Journal of a Tour in Ireland.* London: W. Miller, 1807.

Hogan, Edmund. *The Description of Ireland, and the State Thereof in Anno 1598 . . . from MSS Preserved in Clongowes-Ward College.* Dublin: M. H. Gill and Son, 1878.

Holmes, George. *Sketches of Some of the Southern Counties of Ireland, Collected During a Tour in the Autumn, 1797.* London: J. P. Dewick for Longman and Ries et al., 1801.

Inglis, Henry O. *Ireland in 1834: A Journey Throughout Ireland During the Spring, Summer, and Autumn of 1834.* 3d ed. 2 vols. London: Whittaker, 1854.

Johnson, James. *A Tour in Ireland; With Meditations and Reflections.* London: S. Highley, 1844.

Lithgow, William. "Description of Ireland and the Irish, A.D. 1619." In James Hall, *Tour Through Ireland.* Vol. II. London: P. P. Moore, 1813.

Luckombe, Phillip. *A Tour Through Ireland: Wherein the Present State of That Kingdom Is Considered; and the Most Noted Cities, Towns, Seats, Buildings, Loughs, Etc. Described. . . .* London: T. Lowndes and Son, 1783.

Mahaffy, J. P. "Two Early Tours in Ireland [1397, 1517]." *Hermathena*, XL (1914), 1–16.

Martineau, Harriet. *Letters from Ireland.* Reprinted from the *Daily News.* London: J. Chapman, 1852.

Moryson, Fynes. "A Description of Ireland." In *Ireland Under Elizabeth and James the First.* Ed. Henry Morly. London, 1890.

Noel, Baptist W. *Notes of a Short Tour Through the Midland Counties of Ireland in the Summer of 1836, with Observations on the Condition of the Peasantry.* London: J. Nesbit, 1837.

Payne, Robert. *A Briefe Description of Ireland: Made in the Yeere 1589 by Robert Payne unto XXV of His Partners for Whom He Is Undertaker There.* London: printed by Thomas Dawson, 1590.

Rich, Barnabe. *A New Description of Ireland; Wherein Is Described the Disposition of the Irish Whereunto They Are Inclined.* London: Thomas Adams, 1610.

Stead, J. B. *A Fortnight in Ireland.* New York: G. P. Putnam, 1853.

Titmarsh, M. A. (William Makepeace Thackeray). *The Irish Sketch-book.* New York: J. Winchester, 1844.

Trotter, John Bernard. *Walks Through Ireland in the Years 1812, 1814 and 1817; Described in a Series of Letters to an English Gentleman*. London: R. Phillips, 1819.

Twiss, Richard. *A Tour in Ireland in 1775*. Privately published by the author. London, 1776.

Walford, Thomas. *The Scientific Tourist Through Ireland . . . by an Irish Gentleman*. London, 1818.

West, Mrs. Frederic. *A Summer Visit to Ireland in 1846*. London, 1847.

Young, Arthur. *A Tour in Ireland: With General Observations on the Present State of That Kingdom, 1776–1779*. Dublin: Whitestone, 1780.

NEWSPAPERS

Cork Reporter
Evening Mail (Dublin)
Evening Post (Dublin)
Freeman's Journal (Dublin)
Herald (London)
Illustrated London News
The Morning Chronicle (London)
Morning Post (London)

Nation (Dublin)
Northern Star (Leeds)
Northern Whig (Belfast)
The Pilot (Dublin)
Standard (London)
The Times (London)
Tipperary Constitution
United Irishman (Dublin)

JOURNALS

Blackwood's Magazine
Dublin University Magazine
Edinburgh Review
Fraser's Magazine

Gentlemen's Magazine
Punch
Quarterly Review
Westminster Review

SECONDARY SOURCES

Ackerman, Nathan W., and Marie Jahoda. *Anti-Semitism and Emotional Disorder: A Psychoanalytic Interpretation*. New York: Harper and Brothers, 1950.

Adams, J. Stacy. "Reduction of Cognitive Dissonance by Seeking Consonant Information." *Journal of Abnormal and Social Psychology*, XXVI, No. 1 (1961), 74–78.

Adorno, T. W., et al. *The Authoritarian Personality*. 2 vols. New York: Harper and Brothers, 1950.

Adrian, Arthur A. *Mark Lemon, First Editor of Punch.* Norman: University of Oklahoma Press, 1966.

Allport, Gordon. *The Nature of Prejudice.* Garden City, N.Y.: Doubleday, 1958.

Arendt, Hannah. *The Origins of Totalitarianism.* New York: Harcourt, Brace and World, 1968.

Ashley-Montague, M. F. *Concept of Race.* New York: Free Press, 1964.

Aydelotte, William O. "Parties and Issues in Early Victorian England." *Journal of British Studies,* V (1966), 195–214.

Bagehot, Walter. *Biographical Studies.* Ed. Richard Holt Hutton. London: Longmans, Green, 1881.

Balandier, G. "La situation coloniale: approche théorique." *Cahiers internationaux de sociologie,* XI (1961), 44–79.

Baldwin, James. *Go Tell It on the Mountain.* New York: Alfred A. Knopf, 1953.

————. *Notes of a Native Son.* Boston: Beacon Press, 1962.

Barnard, F. P. *Strongbow's Conquest of Ireland, 1166–86.* London: D. Nutt, 1888.

Barzun, Jacques. *Race: A Study in Superstition.* Rev. ed. New York: Harper and Row, 1965.

Bauer, Raymond A. "Accuracy of Perception in International Relations." *Teachers' College Record,* LXIV, No. 4 (1963), 291–299.

Beckett, James Cambin. *The Making of Modern Ireland.* New York: Alfred A. Knopf, 1966.

Black, R. D. Collison. *Economic Thought and the Irish Question, 1817–1870.* Cambridge: Cambridge University Press, 1962.

Blackall, Henry, and J. H. Whyte. "Correspondence on O'Connell and the Repeal Party." *Irish Historical Studies,* XII, No. 46 (September 1960), 139–143.

Blake, R., and W. Dennis. "The Development of Stereotypes Concerning the Negro." *Journal of Abnormal and Social Psychology,* XXXVIII (1943), 525–531.

Blake, Robert. *Disraeli.* London: Eyre and Spottiswoode, 1966.

Bloom, Solomon F. *Ireland's Destiny as It Appeared to Karl Marx.* Irish Committee on Historical Sciences, Bull. No. 46, 1946.

Bolton, Geoffrey C. *The Passing of the Irish Act of Union: A Study in Parliamentary Politics.* London: Oxford University Press, 1966.

Bonn, Moritz Julius. *Die englische Kolonisation in Ireland.* 2 vols. Stuttgart: J. C. Cottasche Buchhandlung Nachfolger, 1906.

Bostrum, Irene. "The Novel and Catholic Emancipation." *Studies in Romanticism,* II, No. 3 (1963), 155–176.

Boulding, Kenneth. *The Image.* Ann Arbor: University of Michigan Press, 1955.

————. "The Learning and Reality-Testing Process in the International System." *Journal of International Affairs,* XXI, No. 1 (1967), 1–15.

Brodbeck, M. "The Role of Small Groups in Mediating the Effects of Propaganda." *Journal of Abnormal Social Psychology,* LII (1956), 166–170.

Broderick, John. *The Holy See and the Irish Movement on the Repeal of the Union with England, 1829–47.* Rome: Universitas Gregoriana, 1951.

Broeker, Galen. "Robert Peel and the Peace Conservation Force." *Journal of Modern History,* XXXIII (1961), 363–373.

Brown, Thomas N. "Nationalism and the Irish Peasant, 1800–48." *Review of Politics,* XV (1953), 403–445.

Burn, W. L. *The Age of Equipoise.* New York: Norton, 1964.

Chapanis, Natalia P. and Alphonse. "Cognitive Dissonance: Five Years Later." *Psychological Bulletin,* LXI, No. 1 (1964), 1–22.

Clapham, J. H. *An Economic History of Modern Britain: The Early Railway Age, 1820–1850.* Cambridge: Cambridge University Press, 1926.

Clark, G. Kitson. *Peel.* London: Duckworth, 1936.

————. *Peel and the Conservative Party.* 2d ed. London: Frank Cass, 1964.

Clarke, Aidan. *The Old English in Ireland, 1625–42.* London: MacGibbon and Kee, 1966.

Clarke, Randall. "The Relations Between O'Connell and the Young Irelanders." *Irish Historical Studies,* II, No. 9 (1942–1943), 18–31.

Clarke, Robert B., and Donald T. Campbell. "A Demonstration of Bias in Estimates of Negro Ability." *Journal of Abnormal and Social Psychology,* LI (1955), 585–588.

Cole, G. D. H. *Ideas and Beliefs of the Victorians.* Ed. Harman Grisewood. London: Sylvan Press, 1949.

Connell, K. H. *The Population of Ireland, 1750–1854.* Oxford: Oxford University Press, 1950.

Connolly, James. *Labour in Irish History.* London: Maunsel, 1917.

Cooper, E., and M. Jahoda. "The Evasion of Propaganda: How Prejudiced People Respond to Anti-Prejudice Propaganda." *Journal of Psychology,* XXIII (1947), 15–25.

Covington, F. F., Jr. "Elizabethan Notions of Ireland." *Texas Review* (Austin), VI (1921), 222–246.

Crespi, Leo P. "Some Observations on the Concept of Image." *Public Opinion Quarterly,* XXV, No. 1 (1961), 115–120.

Cromwell, Valerie. "Interpretations of Nineteenth-Century Administration: An Analysis." *Victorian Studies,* IX (1966), 245–255.

Crosland, Thomas William Hodgson. *The Wild Irishman.* London: T. Werner Laurie, 1905.

Curtis, L. P., Jr. *The Anglo-Saxons and Celts: A Study of Anti-Irish Prejudice in Victorian England.* Bridgeport, Conn.: Conference on British Studies, 1968.

———. *Apes and Angels: The Irishman in Victorian Caricature.* Washington, D.C.: Smithsonian Institution Press, 1971.

Dance, Ernest Herbert. *The Victorian Illusion.* London: W. Heinemann, 1928.

Davies, J. Conway. "Giraldus Cambrensis, 1146–1946." *Archaeologia Cambrensis,* XCIX (1946), 85–108.

Davis, Herbert, ed. *The Prose Works of Jonathan Swift.* 13 vols. Oxford: Shakespeare Head Press, 1939–1962.

Dekker, Edward Douwes. *Max Havelaar, or The Coffee Sales of the Netherlands Trading Company.* Trans. W. Siebenhaar. New York: Alfred A. Knopf, 1927.

de Lavergne, Léonce. *Essai sur l'économie rurale de l'Angleterre, de l'Écosse et de l'Irlande.* 3d ed. Paris, 1858.

Deutsch, Karl. *Nationalism and Social Communication.* Cambridge, Mass.: M.I.T. Press, 1953.

———. *The Nerves of Government.* New York: Free Press, 1963.

Deutsch, Karl, et al. *Political Community and the North Atlantic Area.* Princeton: Princeton University Press, 1957.

Diab, Lufty N. "Factors Affecting Studies of National Stereotypes." *Journal of Social Psychology*, LIX, No. 1 (1963), 29–40.

———. "National Stereotypes and the 'Reference Group' Concept." *Journal of Social Psychology*, LVII (1962), 339–351.

Duffy, Charles Gavan. *Four Years of Irish History*. London: Cassell, Pelter, Golpin, 1883.

———. *Young Ireland: A Fragment of Irish History*. London: T. Fisher Unwin, 1896.

Dunlop, Robert. "Some Aspects of Henry VIII's Irish Policy." In *Historical Essays by Members of the Owens College*. London, 1902.

Easton, Stewart C. *The Twilight of European Colonialism*. London: Methuen, 1961.

Edwards, R. Dudley, and T. Desmond Williams, eds. *The Great Famine*. New York: New York University Press, 1957.

Ehrlich, Howard J. "Stereotyping and Negro-Jewish Stereotypes." *Social Forces*, XLI, No. 2 (1962), 171–176.

Emerson, Rupert. *From Empire to Nation*. Cambridge, Mass.: Harvard University Press, 1960.

Eversley, George John Shaw. *Peel and O'Connell: A Review of the Irish Policy of Parliament from the Act of Union to the Death of Sir Robert Peel*. London: Kegan Paul, Trench, 1887.

Faber, Richard. *The Vision and the Need: Late Victorian Imperialist Aims*. London: Faber and Faber, 1966.

Falls, Cyril Bentham. *Elizabeth's Irish Wars*. London: Methuen, 1950.

Fanon, Frantz. *The Wretched of the Earth*. Trans. Constance Farrington. New York: Grove Press, 1963.

Ferguson, Oliver W. *Jonathan Swift and Ireland*. Urbana: University of Illinois Press, 1962.

Festinger, Leon. *A Theory of Cognitive Dissonance*. Stanford: Stanford University Press, 1952.

Festinger, Leon, et al. *Conflict, Decision, and Dissonance*. Stanford: Stanford University Press, 1964.

Fishman, Joshua A. "An Examination of the Process and Function of Social Stereotyping." *Journal of Social Psychology*, XLIII (1956), 27–64.

Forster, E. M. *A Passage to India*. New York: Harcourt, Brace, 1924.

Freeman, T. W. *Pre-Famine Ireland.* Manchester: Manchester University Press, 1957.

Freud, Sigmund. "Further Remarks on the Neuro-Psychoses of Defense." In *The Standard Edition of the Complete Psychological Works of Sigmund Freud.* London: Hogarth Press, 1962.

———. "The Neuro-Psychoses of Defense." In *The Standard Edition of the Complete Psychological Works of Sigmund Freud.* London: Hogarth Press, 1962.

Fromm, Eric. *Escape from Freedom.* New York: Farrar and Rinehart, 1941.

Froude, James A. "Romanism and the Irish Race." *North American Review,* January 1880.

Gash, Norman. *Mr. Secretary Peel.* London: Longmans, 1961.

———. *Reaction and Reconstruction in English Politics, 1832–1852.* Oxford: Oxford University Press, 1965.

Gill, C. *The Rise of the Irish Linen Industry.* Oxford: Oxford University Press, 1925.

Glass, David V., ed. *Population in History: Essays in Historical Demography.* London: E. Arnold, 1965.

Gooch, George Peabody. "Great Britain and Ireland, 1792–1815." In *Cambridge Modern History.* Vol. IX. Cambridge: Cambridge University Press, 1906.

Gordon, Rosemary. *Stereotypy of Imagery and Belief.* Cambridge: Cambridge University Press, 1962.

Gorer, Geoffrey. "Le concept de caractère national." *Revue de psychologie des peuples,* XIV (May 1946), 236–252.

Gosset, Thomas F. *Race: The History of an Idea in America.* Dallas: Southern Methodist University Press, 1963.

Green, E. R. R. "The Cotton Hand-loom Weavers in the Northeast of Ireland." *Ulster Journal of Archaeology* (Belfast), VII (1944), 30–41.

Greene, Graham. *The Heart of the Matter.* London: W. Heinemann, 1948.

Gwynn, Denis. "England: The Famine and the Church in England." *Irish Ecclesiastical Record,* LXIX, 896–909.

———. *Young Ireland and 1848.* Cork: Cork University Press, 1949.

Halévy, Elie. *A History of the English People in the Nineteenth Century.* Trans. E. I. Watkin. 6 vols. New York: Barnes and Noble, 1961.

Hart, Jenifer. "Sir Charles Trevelyan at the Treasury." *English Historical Review,* LXXV (1960), 92–110.

Hastorf, A., and H. Cantril. "They Saw a Game: A Case Study." *Journal of Abnormal and Social Psychology,* XLIX (1954), 129–134.

Henley, Pauline. *Spenser in Ireland.* Cork: Cork University Press, 1928.

Hennig, John. "Dickens in Ireland." *Irish Monthly,* LXXV, 248–255.

Hinton, Edward Martin. *Ireland Through Tudor Eyes.* Philadelphia: University of Pennsylvania Press, 1935.

Hodgkin, Thomas. *Nationalism in Colonial Africa.* Fair Lawn, N.J.: Essential Books, 1956.

Holsti, Ole R. "Cognitive Dynamics and Images of the Enemy." *International Affairs,* XXI, No. 1 (1967), 16–39.

Horn, David. *British Public Opinion and the First Partition of Poland.* Edinburgh and London: Oliver and Boyd, 1945.

Inglis, Brian. "O'Connell and the Irish Press, 1800–42." *Irish Historical Studies,* XIII, No. 29 (March 1952), 1–28.

Isaacs, Harold R. *Images of Asia: American Views of China and India.* New York: Capricorn Books, 1962.

Jackson, J. A. "The Irish in Britain." *Sociological Review,* n.s., X (1962), 5–16.

Judson, Alexander C. *The Life of Edmund Spenser.* Baltimore: Johns Hopkins Press, 1945.

———. *Spenser in Southern Ireland.* Bloomington, Ind.: Principia Press, 1933.

Kaplan, Morton. *System and Process in International Relations.* New York: John Wiley, 1957.

Kennan, George F. "The Sources of Soviet Conduct." *Foreign Affairs,* XXV (1947), 561.

Kennedy, Brian A. "William Sharman Crawford: A Political Biography." Completed dissertation. Belfast: Queens University, 1953.

Kleiger, Samuel. "Spenser's Irish Tract and Tribal Democracy." *South Atlantic Quarterly,* XLIX (1950), 490–497.

Klineberg, Otto. "The Scientific Study of National Stereotypes." *International Social Science Bulletin*, III (1951), 511–512.

Kosa, John. "The Rank Order of People: A Study in National Stereotypes." *Journal of Social Psychology*, November 1957, 311–320.

Kuhn, Theodore S. *The Structure of Scientific Revolutions*. Chicago: University of Chicago Press, 1962.

Langer, William. *The Diplomacy of Imperialism*. New York: Alfred A. Knopf, 1960.

Large, David. "The House of Lords and Ireland in the Age of Peel, 1832–50." *Irish Historical Studies*, IX, No. 36 (September 1955), 367–400.

La Violette, Forest, and K. H. Silvert. "A Theory of Stereotypes." *Social Forces*, XXIX (1950), 257–262.

Lebow, Richard Ned. "British Historians and Irish History." *Éire-Ireland*, VIII (December 1973), 3–38.

———. "British Images of Poverty in Pre-Famine Ireland." In Daniel Casey and Richard Rhodes, eds., *The Irish Peasant in the Nineteenth Century* (forthcoming).

Lecky, W. E. H. *The Leaders of Public Opinion in Ireland: Swift—Flood—Grattan—O'Connell.* 2 vols. London: Longmans, 1903.

Lenin, V. I. *Imperialism: The Highest Stage of Capitalism.* New York: International Publishers, 1939.

Levack, Paul. "Edmund Burke, His Friends, and the Dawn of the Irish-Catholic Emancipation." *Catholic Historical Review*, XXXVII (1952), 393.

Levy, Richard. *Anti-Semitic Political Parties in the German Empire.* New Haven: Yale University Press, 1969.

Levy-Bruhl, Lucien. *The "Soul" of the Primitive.* Trans. Lilian Clare. London: George Allen and Unwin, 1928.

Lewis, George Cornwall. *On Local Disturbances in Ireland; and on the Irish Church Question.* London: B. Fellowes, 1836.

Lippmann, Walter. *Public Opinion.* Rev. ed. New York: Macmillan, 1960.

Lipson, Ephraim. *The Economic History of England.* 6th ed. 3 vols. London: Adam and Charles Black, 1956.

McCaffrey, Lawrence J. "Isaac Butt and the Home Rule Movement: A Study in Conservative Nationalism." *Review of Politics* (Notre Dame), XXII (1960), 72–95.

MacCartney, Donald. "The Writing of History in Ireland, 1800–30." *Irish Historical Studies*, X, No. 40 (September 1957), 347–363.

Maccoby, Simon. *English Radicalism, 1832–1852.* London: George Allen and Unwin, 1935.

McDowell, Robert Brendan. *The Irish Administration, 1801–1914.* London: Routledge and Kegan Paul, 1964.

――――. *Irish Public Opinion, 1750–1800.* London: Faber and Faber, 1944.

――――. *Public Opinion and Government Policy in Ireland, 1801–1846.* London: Faber and Faber, 1952.

McGaughy, David J. "Irish Education in the Nineteenth Century." *Irish Universities Historical Congress Bulletin*, V, 33–40.

McGrath, Kevin M. "Writers in the 'Nation,' 1842–45." *Irish Historical Studies*, VI, No. 23 (March 1949), 189–224.

Machin, G. I. T. "The Catholic Emancipation Crisis of 1825." *English Historical Review*, LXXVIII, 458–482.

――――. *The Catholic Question in English Politics, 1820 to 1830.* Oxford: Clarendon Press, 1964.

Macintyre, Angus. *The Liberator: Daniel O'Connell and the Irish Party, 1830–1847.* New York: Macmillan, 1965.

MacManus, M. J. *Thomas Davis and Young Ireland.* Dublin: Stationery Office, 1945.

Mahoney, Thomas H. D. *Edmund Burke and Ireland.* Cambridge, Mass.: Harvard University Press, 1960.

Majundar, R. C. "Nationalist Historians." In C. H. Phillips, ed., *Historians of India, Pakistan and Ceylon.* London: Oxford University Press, 1961.

Mandle, W. F. *Anti-Semitism and the British Union of Fascists.* London: Longmans, 1968.

Mannoni, Octave. *Prospero and Caliban (Psychologie de la colonisation).* Trans. Pamela Powesland. New York: Praeger, 1964.

Mansergh, Nicholas. *Britain and Ireland.* Rev. ed. London: Longmans, Green, 1946.

————. *The Irish Question, 1840–1921.* Toronto: University of Toronto Press, 1965.

Mansur, Fatma. *Process of Independence: A Study of the Political Process in India, Pakistan, Indonesia, and Ghana.* New York: Humanities Press, 1962.

Maunier, René. *The Sociology of the Colonies: An Introduction to the Study of a Race Contact.* Trans. and ed. E. O. Lorimer. 2 vols. London: Kegan Paul, 1949.

Memmi, Albert. *The Colonizer and the Colonized.* New York: Orion Books, 1965.

————. *Portrait d'un juif l'impasse.* Paris: Gallimard, 1962.

————. *La statue de sel.* Paris: Gallimard, 1966.

Merton, Robert K. "The Self-Fulfilling Prophecy." *Antioch Review,* VIII (1948), 193–210.

Mill, James. *The History of British India.* 3 vols. London: Baldwin, Cradock, and Joy, 1817.

Mills, J., E. Aronson, and H. Robinson. "Selectivity in Exposure to Information." *Journal of Abnormal and Social Psychology,* LIX (1959), 250–253.

Misra, R. K. "An Examination of the Concept of Stereotypes." *Psychological Studies* (Mysore, India), IX, No. 1 (1964), 52–57.

Monteil, V. "La décolonisation de la histoire." *Preuves,* CXLII, (1962), 3–12.

Mooney, Canice. "The Beginnings of the Irish Language Revival." *Irish Ecclesiastical Review,* LXIV, 10–18.

Mordaunt. *Sketches of Life, Characters and Manners in Various Countries.* Ed. R. C. Renwick. London: Oxford University Press, 1965.

Morison, Stanley. *History of The Times.* Vols. I and II. (Originally published in 1835–1852.) London: The Times, 1939.

Murray, R. H. *Revolutionary Island and Its Settlement.* London: Macmillan, 1911.

Myrdal, Gunnar, et al. *An American Dilemma: The Negro Problem and Modern Democracy.* New York: Harper and Brothers, 1944.

Nicolson, William (Archbishop of Cashel). *The Irish Historical Library.* Dublin: R. Owen, 1724.

Norman, Montagu. *The Catholic Church in Ireland in the Age of Revolution, 1859–1903.* London: Longmans, Green, 1965.

Nowlan, Kevin B. *Charles Gavan Duffy and the Repeal Movement.* Dublin: National University of Ireland, 1963.

————. "The Meaning of Repeal in Irish History." Reprinted from *Historical Studies*, IV. London: Bowes and Bowes, 1963.

————. *The Politics of Repeal: A Study in the Relations Between Great Britain and Ireland, 1841–1850.* London: Routledge and Kegan Paul, 1965.

————. "Writings in Connection with Thomas Davis and the Young Ireland Centenary, 1948." *Irish Historical Studies*, V (1947), 265–272.

O'Brien, R. Barry. *Parliamentary History of the Irish Land Question from 1829 to 1869; and the Origin and Results of the Ulster Custom.* London: Sampson, Low, Marston, Searle and Rivington, 1880.

O'Brien, Conor Cruise. *The Shaping of Modern Ireland.* London: Routledge and Kegan Paul, 1960.

O'Brien, George. *History of Ireland from the Union to the Famine.* London: Longmans, 1921.

O'Connell, Maurice R. *Irish Politics and Social Conflict in the Age of the American Revolution.* Philadelphia: University of Pennsylvania Press, 1965.

O'Connor, G. *Elizabethan Ireland, Native and English.* Dublin: Sealy, Bryers and Walker, 1906.

O'Rahilly, Alfred. "The Irish University Question." *Studies*, L (1961), 353–370.

O'Rahilly, Thomas Francis. *Early Irish History and Mythology.* Dublin: Dublin Institute for Advanced Studies, 1946.

O'Rourke, John. *The History of the Great Irish Famine of 1847, with Notice of Earlier Famines.* Dublin: M'Glashan and Gill, 1875.

Orpen, Goddard Henry. *Ireland Under the Normans.* 4 vols. Oxford: Oxford University Press, 1911–1920.

Orwell, George. *Burmese Days.* London: Victor Gollancz, 1935.

Parker, James. *Anti-Semitism.* Chicago: Quadrangle, 1964.

Pierrard, Pierre. *Juifs et catholiques français, de Drumont à Jules Isaac (1886–1945).* Paris: Fayard, 1970.

Pomfret, John E. *The Struggle for Land in Ireland, 1800–1923*. Princeton: Princeton University Press, 1930.

Price, Richard G. G. *A History of Punch*. London: Collins, 1957.

Prothro, E. T. "Studies in Stereotypes: V. Familiarity and the Kernel of Truth Hypothesis." *Journal of Social Psychology*, XLI (1955), 3–10.

Quinn, David Beers. "Edward Walshe's 'Conjectures' [1552] Concerning the State of Ireland." *Irish Historical Studies*, V, No. 2 (September 1947), 303–323.

——. *The Elizabethans and the Irish*. Ithaca, N.Y.: Cornell University Press (for the Folger Shakespeare Library), 1966.

Rapoport, Anatol. *Fights, Games and Debates*. Ann Arbor: University of Michigan Press, 1960.

——. *Strategy and Conscience*. New York: Harper and Row, 1964.

Reigrotski, Erich and Anderson. "National Stereotypes and Foreign Contacts." *Public Opinion Quarterly*, XXIII, No. 4 (1959), 515–528.

Reilly, Sister M. Paracleta. *Aubrey de Vere, Victorian Observer*. Lincoln: University of Nebraska Press, 1953.

Reynolds, James A. *The Catholic Emancipation Crisis in Ireland, 1823–1829*. New Haven: Yale University Press, 1954.

Salaman, Redcliffe N. *The Influence of the Potato on the Course of Irish History*. Cambridge: Cambridge University Press, 1949.

Sanders, Charles-Richard. "Retracing Carlyle's Irish Journey." *Studies*, L (1961), 38–50.

Sartre, Jean Paul. *Portrait of the Anti-Semite*. London: Secker and Warburg, 1948.

Schelling, Thomas. *Arms and Influence*. New Haven: Yale University Press, 1966.

——. *Strategy of Conflict*. Cambridge, Mass.: Harvard University Press, 1963.

Schumpeter, Joseph. *Imperialism and Social Classes*. Trans. Heinz Norden. New York: A. M. Kelley, 1951.

Shaw, George Bernard. *John Bull's Other Island*. London: Archibald Constable, 1909.

Shaw, Nessan. "The Problem of Intemperance in Ireland, 1838–56." *Irish Commission Historical Society Bulletin*, No. 39 (1945).

Shrieke, B. *Alien Americans.* New York: Viking, 1936.

Snyder, Richard, H. W. Bruck, and Burton Sapin. *Foreign Policy Decision-Making: An Approach to the Study of International Relations.* New York: Free Press, 1962.

Solomon, Barbara. *Ancestors and Immigrants: A Changing New England Tradition.* Cambridge, Mass.: Harvard University Press, 1956.

Spielmann, M. H. *The History of Punch.* New York: Cassell, 1895.

Stoessinger, John G. "China and America: The Burden of Past Misperceptions." *Journal of International Affairs* (New York), XXI, No. 1 (1967), 72–92.

Strauss, Eric. *Irish Nationalism and British Democracy.* New York: Columbia University Press, 1951.

Thornley, David. *Isaac Butt and Home Rule.* London: MacGibbon and Kee, 1964.

Thornton, Archibald Paton. *The Imperial Idea and Its Enemies: A Study in British Power.* London: Macmillan, 1959.

Tierney, Michael, ed. *Daniel O'Connell: Mid-Centenary Essays.* Dublin: Brown and Nolan, 1949.

Wall, Maureen. "The Rise of a Catholic Middle Class in Eighteenth-Century Ireland." *Irish Historical Studies*, XI, No. 42 (September 1958), 91–116.

Walpole, Spencer. *The Life of Lord John Russell.* 2 vols. London: Longmans, Green, 1889.

Waterhouse, Gilbert. "Fynes Moryson, Traveler." *Irish Committee on Historical Sciences Bulletin*, No. 36 (1945).

Weston, John C., Jr. "Edmund Burke's Irish History: A Hypothesis." *Publications of the Modern Language Association*, LXXVII (1962), 397–403.

Whyte, J. H. "Daniel O'Connell and the Repeal Party." *Irish Historical Studies*, XI, No. 44 (September 1959), 297–317.

———. "The Influence of the Catholic Clergy on Elections in Nineteenth Century Ireland." *English Historical Review*, No. 295 (April 1960), 239–259.

Williams, T. F. Desmond. *The Attitude of British Statesmen and British Public Opinion Towards Irish National Movements, 1830–80.* Doctoral dissertation. University College (Dublin), 1945.

Wilson, J. M. "Statistics of Crime in Ireland, 1842 to 1850." *Journal of the Dublin Statistical Society*, II, Part X (November 1857).

Woodham-Smith, Cecil. *The Great Hunger.* New York: Harper and Row, 1962.

Woodward, C. Vann. *The Strange Career of Jim Crow.* New York: Oxford University Press, 1955.

Woodward, Llewellyn. *The Age of Reform: 1815–1870.* 2d ed. rev. Oxford: Oxford University Press, 1962.

Wright, Richard. *Native Son.* New York: Harper and Brothers, 1940.

Young, G. M., ed. *Early Victorian England, 1830–1865.* 2 vols. London: Oxford University Press, 1934.

Zaidi, S. M. Hafeez. "National Stereotypes of University Students in Pakistan." *Journal of Social Psychology*, LXIII, No. 1 (1964), 73–85.

BIBLIOGRAPHIES AND GENERAL REFERENCES

BIBLIOGRAPHIES

Abbott, T. K. *Catalogue of Fifteenth-Century Books in the Library of Trinity College, Dublin, and in Marsh's Library, Dublin, with a Few from Other Collections.* Dublin: Hodges, Figgis, 1905.

Condon, John. *A Short Bibliography of Irish History: Hanover Period, Part I (1714–1803).* Dublin: Browne and Nolan, 1909.

Eager, Alan R. *A Guide to Irish Bibliographical Material.* London: Library Association, 1964.

Haig, James D. *A List of Books Printed in England Prior to the Year MDC, in the Library of . . . the King's Inns, Dublin.* Dublin, 1858.

Hayes, Richard J., ed. *Manuscript Sources for the History of Irish Civilization.* Boston: Hall, 1965.

Houghton, Walter E., ed. *The Wellesley Index to Victorian Periodicals, 1824–1900.* Vol. I. Toronto: University of Toronto Press, 1960.

Irish Historical Studies (The Joint Journal of the Irish Historical Society and the Ulster Society for Irish Historical Studies). *Annual Bibliography*, Vol. I, No. 1 (March 1938).

New York Public Library. *List of Works in the New York Public Library Relating to Ireland.* New York, 1905.

Ramage, David, compiler. *A Finding List of English Books to 1640 in Libraries of the British Isles, Based on the Numbers in Pollard and Redgman's "Short-Title Catalogue."* Durham: G. Bailes and Sons, 1958.

Templeman, William D., ed. *Bibliographies of Studies in Victorian Literature for the Thirteen Years, 1932–44.* Urbana: University of Illinois, 1945.

GENERAL REFERENCES

Battersby's Register for the Catholic World, or The Complete Catholic Directory, Almanac and Registry. . . . Dublin, 1836.

Dod's Parliamentary Pocket Companion. Published annually. London: Whittaker, Treacher and Arnot, 1833–1850.

The Dublin Almanac and General Register of Ireland. Dublin: Pettigrew and Oulton, 1840–1850.

Stephen, Leslie, and Sidney Lee, eds. *Dictionary of National Biography.* London: Oxford University Press, 1921–1927.

Thom's Irish Almanac and Official Directory. Dublin: Alexander Thom and Sons, 1840–1850.

Index